Elizabeth I

AND HER WORLD

Elizabeth I

AND HER WORLD

SUSAN WATKINS

PHOTOGRAPHS BY MARK FIENNES

With 157 illustrations, 154 in color

For Dr Elizabeth Jacobs and Miss Alyce Nash, Liz and Sandy,
with love, always, and gratitude for teaching me to see with my heart.

The photographs on the following pages are by
Mark Fiennes: 5, 9, 10, 11, 12, 13, 18, 25, 26, 28,
30, 31, 36, 40, 43, 44–5, 48, 49, 52, 53, 58, 59, 60,
66, 67, 70–1, 71, 80 (TOP), 87, 88, 91, 94, 102,
103, 104–5, 105, 106, 107, 108 (BOTTOM), 109,
110, 111, 112, 113, 115, 116 (RIGHT), 123, 124–5,
126–7, 128, 129, 131, 133, 134, 135, 136, 137,
138, 139, 140, 141, 142, 143, 144, 145, 146, 147,
151, 155, 165, 168, 169, 170, 180, 182–3, 184–5,
186, 187, 192, 193, 196, 198–9. All other
illustration credits can be found on page 204.

First published in 1998 in hardcover in the
United States of America, under the title
The Public and Private Worlds of Elizabeth I, by
Thames & Hudson Inc., 500 Fifth Avenue,
New York, New York 10110
thamesandhudsonusa.com

First paperback edition 2007

Library of Congress Catalog Card Number
2007924444
ISBN 978-0-500-28695-1

Printed and bound in Singapore by CS Graphics

Frontispiece and title page The *Ermine
Portrait*, traditionally attributed to Nicholas
Hilliard. This life-size portrait, dated 1585,
is typical of the lavish representations of
Elizabeth showing her as the virtuous Virgin
Queen. She wears a gem-embroidered gown
and strings of jewels. From a collar of
diamond and pearls hangs the famous royal
jewel known as 'The Three Brothers', which
consists of three oblong diamonds set around
a pointed diamond and separated by pearls.
A single, large, tear-shaped pearl is suspended
below. Visible on Elizabeth's left arm is an
ermine, a symbol of purity and virginity.
On a table next to her is the Sword of State,
symbolizing Justice, and in her hand a sprig of
olive, symbolizing Peace. The painting is now
at Hatfield House in Hertfordshire.

Opposite An exterior detail of Wollaton
Hall in Nottinghamshire, built between 1580
and 1588.

Contents

Opposite and above
The *Ditchley Portrait*
by Marcus Gheeraerts
the Younger. Rarely
in art has there been
a more explicit fusion
of monarch and
kingdom. The
painting was probably
produced in
connection with the
lavish entertainments
organized for
Elizabeth by her
devoted courtier and
champion Sir Henry
Lee at his home at
Ditchley, Oxfordshire,
in 1592. It symbolizes
the Queen's authority
over her country:
England is literally at
her feet, with one foot
near Ditchley. From
Elizabeth's left ear
hangs an ornament in
the shape of a celestial
sphere, a symbol of
divine power.

Preface

On 15 January 1559, the Crown of England was placed upon Elizabeth Tudor's head. During her reign of more than forty-four years, England was transformed from an undisciplined backwater into a nation respected by the world. It was a transformation achieved by love. With intuitive genius, Elizabeth understood the needs of her subjects, and responded to those needs by promoting an image of herself specifically tailored to evoke devotion. In a male-orientated society divided by religion, she became the Virgin Queen, a goddess from the heavens bringing to Earth a second golden age. While remaining the country's chaste goddess, she also assumed variations of the myth – Diana, Cynthia, Pandora, Belphoebe, Astraea, Oriana, Gloriana – eventually becoming a celestial being at one with the cosmos, though remarkably and irresistibly never losing the human touch. Along with these images went a form of personal management that operated above the fray – involved, yet vacillating – with a vagueness that confounded reaction, thereby allowing the promise of a golden age to become a reality: under Elizabeth, England was peaceful and prospered. The success of her rule by 'love-tricks' was also evident culturally: in the various portraits of the Queen that appeared in households across the land; in the people's wearing of the royal image cut into cameos or engraved on medallions; in plays, pageants, literature and architecture; and in the decoration of interiors and gardens – to love Elizabeth was to love England. Elizabeth Tudor not only personalized an era, she personalized a national style.

But what about the private woman who exchanged the comparatively subdued surroundings of her girlhood for the opulence of royal palaces and the taut atmosphere of Court? The palaces were adapted to suit the taste of an overtly feminine monarch, but there were few additions in bricks and mortar, since maintenance of the country's finances did not permit an extravagant building programme. Elizabeth did, however, commission minor building works, new windows to overlook her flower garden, and endless repairs. A banqueting house she had constructed at Whitehall Palace was the most significant new building. A fairy-tale edifice of 292 windows and a ceiling painted with stars, the sun, clouds and sunbeams, and hung with flowers, foliage and every 'manner of strange fruits' all glistening with gold, the banqueting house had been built to entertain commissioners from France who were negotiating marriage between Elizabeth and Francis, Duke of Alençon, seemingly the only man she ever intended to marry. The building at Whitehall was frivolous, luxurious, but also refined – so like Elizabeth and her Court. Amongst her courtiers she delighted in playing the coquette. Her favourites received a larger measure of affection and royal bounty; more was expected in return. The tokens of courtiers' devotion took the form of lavish jewels encoded with symbolism, legendary entertainments, and palaces that awaited Her Majesty's grace. They also created gardens combining terraces, canals, mounts and statuary, all for the honour of Elizabeth. The private love expressed for a virtuous lady fused with the public love of a Virgin Queen, creating a unique style of adulation. In these pages, we explore some of its features – the anatomy of a love-spell.

Opposite An oak tree in the grounds of Elvetham in Hampshire. The tree was reputedly planted by Elizabeth in 1591 when she visited the house, the country residence of the Earl of Hertford, during one of her regular summer progresses.

Left Three-day-old Princess Elizabeth may have been dressed in this long silk-and-lace robe for her christening ceremony at Greenwich Palace in September 1533. The robe, from the collection of Emma Dent, was authenticated during the nineteenth century, and is now at Sudeley Castle in Gloucestershire.

Sweet Sister Temperance

*'In adornment she is elegant rather
than showy … I teach her words and
she [teaches] me things'*

(Roger Ascham, Elizabeth's tutor)

Above Wall panels, thought to be from Nonsuch palace in Surrey, showing the initials and portcullis emblem of Elizabeth's father King Henry VIII. The middle panel bears a maiden's head rising from a Tudor rose, the device of Henry's sixth and last wife Katherine Parr, who became very close to her stepdaughter Elizabeth. The panels are now in the great hall at Loseley Hall (Loseley Park), Surrey.

On 7 September 1533, a princess was born at Greenwich Palace, in a bed so 'magnificent' and 'gorgeous' it had once formed part of the ransom of a French nobleman. Three days later, the princess was christened Elizabeth. What should have been a joyous event for the child's parents – King Henry VIII and his second wife Anne Boleyn – was a bitter disappointment. Henry needed a male heir to secure the future of England, and Anne needed a son to secure her continued existence. A joust that had been planned to celebrate the birth of a prince was immediately cancelled. The christening ceremony, however, was allowed to go ahead with all the stateliness accorded a royal birth. The walls between the palace and the Chapel of the Observant Friars, where the christening was held, were hung with tapestries, and the way was strewn with green rushes. The procession set forward from the great hall:

First the citizens, two and two; then Gentlemen, Esquires and Chaplains; next after them the Aldermen, and the Mayor alone, and next the King's Council; then the King's Chapel, in copes; then Barons, Bishops, Earls; the Earl of Essex, bearing the covered gilt basins; after him the Marquess of Exeter with a taper of virgin wax; next [to] him the Marquess [of] Dorset, bearing the salt; behind him the Lady Mary of Norfolk, bearing the Chrisom [a white cloth put upon the child after the ceremony], which was very rich of pearl and stone.

The Duchess of Norfolk carried the child in a mantle of purple velvet with a long train edged with ermine, and the Countess of Kent held the train of the child's mantle, followed by many ladies and gentlewomen. Only King Henry was absent: he could not bring himself to attend the ceremony. Having divorced his first wife Catherine of Aragon in order to marry Anne Boleyn – thereby severing himself and England from the Church of Rome – he had achieved only

Above A cut-work bedcover attributed during the nineteenth century to Anne Boleyn, and thought to have been made for her daughter Elizabeth. Needlework was a favourite pastime of the ladies of the Court, and Elizabeth showed considerable skill at embroidery. The bedcover, from the collection of Emma Dent, is now at Sudeley Castle.

Left and opposite A portrait of Anne Boleyn painted by an unknown artist sometime after her marriage to Henry VIII in 1533. The Queen wears a pearl necklace, from which hang Anne and Henry's initials fashioned from gold. The portrait is now at Loseley Hall.

a daughter. Thomas Cranmer, Archbishop of Canterbury, who had helped prepare the way for the King's divorce, was the child's godfather. The godmothers were the Duchess of Norfolk and the Marchioness of Dorset. The baby was brought to the font and christened, and the Garter Chief King of Arms cried aloud: 'God of his infinite goodness send prosperous life and long to the high and mighty Princess of England Elizabeth!'

Although Anne Boleyn had yearned for a son, she seems to have taken enough interest in her daughter to dress her in regal style. According to the Queen's accounts, there were purchases of orange and russet velvet, white damask and yellow satin to be made up for the baby's kirtles (skirts, or jackets with skirts attached), and there were caps of white, crimson and purple satin embroidered with gold. One cap travelled by boat from Greenwich to London for a fitting, and made another journey when it needed a repair. But neither the young princess's status nor her wardrobe were to last. In 1536, Anne Boleyn was accused of adultery, incest and conspiracy to murder the King. When Elizabeth was two years and eight months old, her mother was beheaded at the Tower of London. The day after the execution, Henry was betrothed to Jane Seymour, and two months later Anne Boleyn's marriage to Henry VIII was pronounced invalid by Archbishop Cranmer. Thus Elizabeth, like her elder half-sister Mary, daughter of Henry's invalidated marriage to Catherine of Aragon, had become illegitimate. Neither daughter was eligible to challenge Henry's future children for the throne. A few months before Anne Boleyn's downfall, Catherine of Aragon had died from natural causes. It was reported that soon after learning of her death, King Henry gave a ball at Greenwich, for which he dressed from head to foot in yellow silk, with a white feather in his cap. During the merrymaking, he clasped two-year-old Elizabeth in his arms, and by candlelight they danced about from room to room as Henry cried out: 'God be praised, the old harridan is dead.'

As was customary for royal children, when Elizabeth was only a few days old she had been given her own household. She was put under the care of Lady Bryan, who had held the post of governess to the royal children for twenty years. Not long after Henry and Elizabeth had danced together at Greenwich, the little girl was outgrowing her clothes. 'She hath neither gown, nor kirtle nor petticoat, nor no manner of linen nor smocks, nor kerchiefs, nor rails [nightdresses], nor body stitchets [corsets], nor biggens [nightcaps]', complained Lady Bryan in a letter to the King's chief minister. 'Now as my Lady Elizabeth is put from that degree she was afore and what degree she is at now I know not

but by hearsay … I know not how to order her, nor myself, nor none of hers that I have the rule of', wrote the governess in the letter, written in the confusing days after Anne Boleyn's death. Furthermore, there was a conflict as to whether or not the child should dine at the board of estate in the great hall – that is, formally, in public, at a great table laid with many dishes – an arrangement Lady Bryan found distressing, for Elizabeth, quite naturally for a toddler, helped herself to adult food: 'divers meats, and fruits and wine'. 'She is yet too young to correct greatly', continued Lady Bryan, who begged that the child be allowed 'a mess of meat at her own lodging, with a good or two that is meet of her grace to eat of'; the remainder of the provisions were to be given to Elizabeth's 'women, a gentleman usher and a groom', eleven persons in all. Lady Bryan also mentioned the strain brought on by Elizabeth's teething, 'which causeth me to suffer her grace to have her will more than I would'. But then, 'she is as toward a child and as gentle of conditions, as ever I knew any in my life'. Despite being 'gentle of conditions', the little girl was not unaware of the alteration in her state of affairs. 'How haps it?', she asked, 'Yesterday my Lady Princess, today but my Lady Elizabeth.'

Lady Bryan wrote her letter from Hunsdon in Hertfordshire, one of several royal houses that had been set aside for use by Henry's children. Before Anne Boleyn's execution, lodgings at Eltham near Greenwich were converted into a nursery for Elizabeth 'on account of the salubrity of the air'. The nursery lodgings comprised a great chamber, a dining chamber, a raying chamber (a dressing room) and a bedchamber. The cradle was lined with crimson satin with a crimson silk fringe, and a leather travelling case was made for it. As well as Eltham and Hunsdon, Elizabeth and her household resided at Hatfield and Ashridge, both in Hertfordshire, the latter being the house mostly associated with the royal children's nursery. Throughout her father's reign, Elizabeth maintained permanent lodgings at Greenwich, the riverside palace east of London rebuilt by her grandfather Henry VII. She was also given lodgings at Hampton Court, the palace built along the Thames by Cardinal Thomas Wolsey, who had presented it, complete with all its costly furniture, tapestries and plate, to Henry VIII in 1525.

One of Elizabeth's earliest public duties took place at Hampton Court in 1537. The occasion was the christening of her half-brother Edward, the son of Jane Seymour, Henry's third wife. Henry had, at last, sired a legitimate male heir: church bells rang out, across the kingdom a jubilant *Te Deum* was sung, bonfires were lit and the poor drank 'as long as they listed'. The joust that had been cancelled after Elizabeth's birth now went ahead.

Prince Edward was christened on 15 October 1537. In the procession, four-year-old Elizabeth carried the chrisom, though to keep pace with the adults she herself had to be carried by the boy's uncle Edward Seymour. Following the ceremony, she assisted Mary and Lady Herbert of Troy in carrying the young prince's train in the procession to the Queen's lodgings. Nine days after the christening, Jane Seymour died of 'child-bed fever'. After her death, Henry allowed a decent interval to pass before marrying his fourth wife, Anne of Cleves, in January 1540. But he could not warm to the 'Flanders Mare' and the marriage ended in divorce the following July. Anne seems to have been fond of Elizabeth, for upon her death seventeen years later, she left jewels to her stepdaughter with the hope that she would employ one of her 'poor' maids. The King's fifth wife was Elizabeth's cousin Katherine Howard, who was beheaded in 1542 following accusations similar to those surrounding Anne Boleyn. Throughout the sequence of stepmothers, Elizabeth's attitude towards her father never wavered: she adored him. And it seems he was always affectionate towards her in return: 'he loves her very much', reported an emissary to the Court. But the King was not above using his daughters to sway public opinion. Soon after his marriage to Jane Seymour, Henry retreated with his bride to Windsor Castle, sending for Mary and Elizabeth to join them, in order to 'soften the temper of the people'.

The death of Edward's mother so soon after his birth was perhaps the beginning of the warm affection that Elizabeth felt for her half-brother. She made him a cambric shirt, and when he was older they exchanged letters in Latin and French. On trying out a new quill, she wrote 'Edwardus' across a page of her writing book. Elizabeth was with Edward for Christmas at Hertford Castle in December 1539 when they were visited by Lord Chancellor Wriothesley with greetings from Henry. The Lord Chancellor reported that six-year-old Lady Elizabeth replied to the King's message 'with as great gravity as she had been forty years old. If she be no worse educated than she now appeareth … she will prove of no less honour to womanhood.' When Edward was six years old and Elizabeth ten, they had lessons together at Hatfield. Like most young ladies of rank during the sixteenth century, Elizabeth was educated to a very high standard in the Renaissance tradition. She was taught Greek and Latin, along with Christian principles. The then centre of influence in education was Cambridge, and specifically Sir John Cheke. Cheke tutored Edward, and to a lesser extent Elizabeth. But it was William Grindal, from the same college as Cheke, St John's, who was responsible for Elizabeth's education until his death in 1548. The famous humanist and scholar Roger Ascham, John Cheke's favourite pupil, then took over the education of Lady Elizabeth. By her tenth year, Elizabeth was learning French and Italian. Her earliest surviving letter was written in Italian in July 1544 to Katherine Parr, Henry's sixth and last wife. Elizabeth had been present at the couple's wedding in 'the Queen's closet' at Hampton Court in the summer of 1543. After the wedding, Elizabeth returned to Hatfield to resume her studies. The style of her Italian letter is formal for a ten-year-old, with grand copybook phrases in the language of the Court. But at the same time the sentiment is unmistakable: Elizabeth was very fond of this previously twice-widowed stepmother who had a gift for maternal nurturing and showed great interest in all of Henry's children. The Queen's round of official duties and Elizabeth's own schedule meant the two had missed seeing each other for a year, a period Elizabeth referred to as her 'exilio'. But Katherine was kept informed of her stepdaughter's progress and well-being through the endless reports and messages that passed between the households. In her letter, Elizabeth also expressed the pride and awe she felt for her father, no doubt mixed with a certain timidness, for by this time Henry had become irascible. She asked Katherine to send the King her wishes for a 'successo bonissimo' in the war in France, during which he captured Boulogne.

Unkind fortune, envious of all good and the continuous whirl of human affairs, has deprived me for a whole year of your most Illustrious presence … This would be unbearable for me, if

Below The young Elizabeth was a talented musician. As well as playing the lute and the virginals (*below*), she also composed and performed her own pieces of music for the pleasure of the Court.

I did not expect to enjoy it again soon. And in this my exile, I know well that in your kindness, your highness has had as much care and solicitude over my health as the King's Majesty. So that I am bound to serve you and to revere you with a daughter's love, since I understand that your most Illustrious Highness has not forgotten me every time you have written to the King's Majesty, which it was my duty to have requested from you, since I have not dared to write to him myself. I now humbly beseech your most Excellent Highness that when you write to his majesty you will recommend me to him, praying always for his sweet blessing and similarly entreating our Lord God to send him best success and the obtaining of victory over his enemies in order that your highness and I may as soon as possible rejoice with him on his happy return …

Elizabeth wrote her Italian letter from the small London palace of St James's. Once a hospital for lepers, it was modernized in 1544, and became the official palace of Prince Edward, although the ceiling of the gatehouse still bore the initials of Elizabeth's parents, 'H' and 'A', lovingly entwined.

For relaxation, there was dancing, riding, hunting, archery and music. Elizabeth played the lute and the virginals; she also enjoyed playing and dancing to her own compositions. And there was always 'work', meaning needlework. By the end of 1544, Elizabeth had finished a translation of the French poem *The Mirror of the Sinful Soul,* written by Marguerite of Navarre, sister of King Francis I of France. It is a serious work which asks, 'Where is the Hell full of travail, pain, mischief, and torment?' The poem was seemingly inappropriate study matter for an eleven-year-old girl: 'But thou hast made separation of my bed and did put thy false lovers in my place and committed fornication with them.' Yet the twenty-seven pages of translation gave the student of French endless exercise, as she said: 'joining the sentences together as well as the capacity of my simple wit and small learning could extend themselves'. Elizabeth's translation is contained in a beautifully embroidered cover made by her for Katherine Parr. In a letter accompanying her gift, Elizabeth explained the poem's theme: 'salvation … be through the grace of God'. She then switched her concern to errors in presentation (presentation would always be paramount):

And although I know that as for my part which I have wrought in it as well spiritual as manual there is nothing done as it should be, nor else worthy to come in your Grace's hands, but rather all unperfect and uncorrect … But I hope that … there shall be nothing in it worthy of reprehension, and that in the meanwhile no other but your Highness only shall read it or see it, lest my faults be known of many.

Above In 1544, eleven-year-old Elizabeth translated the French poem *The Mirror of the Sinful Soul* as a gift for her stepmother Katherine Parr. The translation was bound in blue cloth, which Elizabeth embroidered with silver thread. The Queen's initials 'KP' appear in the centre of an intricate knotwork pattern.

At each of the corners of the cover, which was bound in blue cloth, Elizabeth stitched a single heartsease – a pansy – in purple, yellow and green silk, and in the centre, the Queen's initials 'KP', surrounded by a knotwork pattern. On the spine, she embroidered forget-me-nots. In the language of flowers in the sixteenth century, the heartsease meant 'thoughts', 'think of me' or 'you occupy my mind'; forget-me-nots meant 'true love' or 'affection'.

A month before the King's marriage to Katherine Parr, a new act of Parliament had restored both Elizabeth and Mary to the succession. The Act of Succession of 1543 gave any issue of the King's marriage to Katherine Parr a claim to the throne, after Edward. In the event of Edward's death, and if Henry and Katherine were childless, the Crown went to Mary – with conditions regarding religion – and if she died without issue, it then passed to Elizabeth. Although the Act omitted legitimizing Henry's daughters, the girls were nevertheless treated with the deference accorded regal status at Court, and in the political game of marriage alliances between monarchs, Elizabeth's name was put forward without hesitation. When she was only eleven years old, Cardinal du Bellay, Archbishop of Paris, tried to negotiate a marriage between Elizabeth and the Duke of Orleans, suggesting that the recently captured Boulogne be returned to France as part of her dowry. The following year, Stephen Gardiner, Bishop of Winchester and King Henry's envoy to Rome, tried to bring about a marriage between Elizabeth and Holy Roman Emperor Charles V's son Prince Philip, who eventually became King Philip II of Spain. There had also been a plan to marry her to the Prince of Denmark. When Elizabeth was just a few years old, she had been displayed 'in very rich apparel, in state and triumph as a princess' so that the foreign ambassadors conducting the marriage negotiations were assured of the child's status. Her clothes were then removed so that the dignitaries could also be certain that she was healthy and unblemished.

In the classroom, precocious Elizabeth and her tutor William Grindal pursued new heights of attainment in the classics and contemporary languages, whilst she perfected her hand at writing in an italic style, achieving the visual elegance for which her letters became renowned. In 1545, Elizabeth made a gift for her father of her own translations, in Latin, French and Italian, of Katherine Parr's *Prayers and Meditations,* a work so popular that it was published nineteen times

Above The cover of Elizabeth's translations of Katherine Parr's *Prayers and Meditations*, which Elizabeth embroidered as a gift for her father. The design includes Henry and Katherine's entwined initials surrounded by four white tudor roses.

Opposite An orpharian reputedly made for Elizabeth by John Rose in 1580. The instrument was an improved, six-string version of the lute, the forerunner of the modern guitar.

before the end of the sixteenth century. Elizabeth put her translations into one volume of 117 pages exquisitely bound in crimson cloth, which she embroidered with gold and silver thread combining Henry's and Katherine's initials. At the corners, front and back, Elizabeth stitched four Tudor roses with green leaves and yellow centres. This was also her first use of the brier rose called eglantine, the badge of her grandmother Elizabeth of York, and a symbol of purity that was to remain one of Elizabeth's favourite emblems. She titled her gift *Prayers or meditations by which the mind may be moved to the patient endurance of all the troubles of this life, to the contempt of vain worldly prosperity and to the faithful expectation of eternal bliss, collected from several divine authors by the noble and most holy Lady Katherine, Queen of England, France and Ireland, and translated from the English by the lady Elizabeth.* Her presentation letter – the only existing letter from Elizabeth to Henry – is full of love and admiration. It begins: 'To the most glorious and mighty king Henry VIII … whose every happiness His Majesty's most humble daughter Elizabeth ever prays, and who she entreats to give her his blessing.' He is her 'matchless and most kind father … whom philosophers regard as a god on earth'. She then refers to her translations:

… it seemed fitting to me that this task should be undertaken by myself, your daughter and one who should be not only the imitator of your virtues but also heir to them … But as to what is mine, if there be any error in it yet it may merit pardon on account of my ignorance, my youth, my short time of study and my goodwill, and if it be undistinguished, even though it merit no praise, yet if it be well received it will powerfully incite me to further efforts … Wherefore I do not doubt but that your fatherly goodness and royal foresight will set no lower value on this private labour of my mind than on any other attainment and that you will feel that this holy work which is the more highly to be valued as having been compiled by the Queen your wife, may have its value ever so little enhanced by being translated by your daughter.

About 1545, Henry commissioned a family portrait symbolizing the Tudor dynasty. His enthroned figure beneath a rich canopy dominates the centre ground, and is flanked by eight-year-old Prince Edward on the King's right, and Jane Seymour on his left. The queen at the time was Katherine Parr, who does not appear in the portrait, leaving little doubt about the primary role of the queen consort: to produce a male heir. The group of three are enclosed by pillars, the symbol of imperial power, and beyond the pillars, on the left of the picture stands Princess Mary. On the right and slightly further back stands

Above Henry VIII
commissioned an
unknown artist to
paint this portrait
symbolizing the
Tudor dynasty in
about 1545. The
three close figures of
Henry, Prince
Edward and Edward's
mother Jane Seymour
dominate the
painting, while Mary
and Elizabeth are
shown as being cut
off from the King
and his male heir,
and therefore remote
from power.

Opposite A portrait
of Elizabeth when she
was about thirteen
years old. This may
have been the painting
which she sent to her
half-brother Edward
in 1546–7. She wears
a rich red-brocade
dress, strings of pearls
and fine gold
jewellery. But the
book of devotions in
her hand and the open
volume in the
background suggest
that the young
princess was
concerned with more
than the ostentatious
display of material
possessions. They
indicate that her
interests were both
religious and scholarly.

Elizabeth. Twenty-nine-year-old Mary and twelve-year-old Elizabeth are
dressed in a similar style, wearing dark green and burgundy, in contrast with
Henry's and Jane Seymour's garments of gold and ermine. To the right and
left sides of the painting are open doors leading outside. In the doorway
behind Mary can be seen Jane the Fool, and in the doorway behind Elizabeth,
Jester Will Somers. Behind each of these figures is a glimpse of the gardens
of Whitehall Palace.

Throughout 1546, Henry's health deteriorated and on 28 January 1547, he
died. The Privy Council brought Edward and Elizabeth together to inform
them of their father's death. The nine-year-old boy, now King Edward VI,
rushed into his half-sister's arms and they wept together for several hours,
amazing the Court with the extent of their grief. Henry's will left the succession
to Edward, then in default of heirs to Mary, and then in default of heirs to
Elizabeth. Should Elizabeth fail to marry and die childless, it then fell to the
family of Henry's sister Mary and her daughter Frances. Frances had three
daughters, Jane (Lady Jane Grey), Catherine and Mary. Shortly before Henry's
death, under orders from the Privy Council, Edward was moved from Hatfield
to Hertford Castle, and Elizabeth was moved to the lesser royal house of Enfield
in Hertfordshire, where she had been given chambers and where the children
had spent Christmas together in 1542. The two began a regular correspondence,
much of it in Latin. In one of his letters to Elizabeth, Edward requested a
portrait of his half-sister. The picture he received is probably the one mentioned
in an inventory of his possessions made in 1547: 'a table picture of the Lady

Sweet Sister Temperance

Elizabeth her grace, with a book in her hand, her gown like crimson cloth with works'. The image portrays a reserved, intelligent, thirteen-year-old girl with dark eyes. Her red-gold hair is enhanced with a red coif trimmed with jewels and pearls, the neckline of her red-brocade gown is similarly trimmed, as is her waist; pearls, a symbol of virginity, were to become a regular part of Elizabeth's dress. She wears three rings on the long tapering fingers of her right hand, and one on her left forefinger. In her hands, she holds a book of prayers, with a ribbon and her finger marking a particular point in the text; the background of the painting displays another book lying open – both props suggest a scholarly life. In a letter accompanying the portrait from Hatfield, Elizabeth wrote: 'For the face I grant I might well blush to offer, but for the mind I shall never be ashamed to present.'

Elizabeth lived with Katherine Parr in her stepmother's various mansions at Hanworth, near Hampton Court, at Chelsea, near London, and at Sudeley Castle in Gloucestershire, spending several months at each until the summer of 1548. In April of that year, Elizabeth's first book was published. The work, a revised version of her earlier translation of Marguerite of Navarre's poem, was printed under the title *A Godly Meditacyon on the Cristen Sowle, concernynge a love towardes God and hys Christe, compyled in Frenche by Lady Margarete Quene of Naver and aptly translated into Englysh by the ryght vertuouse Lady Elyzabeth daughter of our late souverayne, Kyng Henri VIII.* The publisher was John Bale, a religious reformer exiled during Henry's reign.

Fifteen-forty-eight was also the year of William Grindal's death. Elizabeth asked for Roger Ascham as a replacement tutor for she was well acquainted with his methods through Grindal. Ascham accepted the position, but resigned at the end of 1549 owing to some conflict in the household. Nevertheless, his influence upon Elizabeth remained great. From the time Elizabeth became queen in November 1558 until Ascham's death nearly ten years later, they read Greek and Latin together almost every day. 'It is difficult to say', Ascham wrote to his friend John Sturm, Rector of the Strasburg Gymnasium, 'whether the gifts of nature or of fortune are most to be admired in my distinguished mistress. The praise which Aristotle gives, wholly centres in her; beauty, stature, prudence and industry.... She talks French and Italian as well as she does English, and has often talked to me readily and well in Latin, moderately in Greek. When she writes Greek and Latin, nothing is more beautiful than her handwriting. She delights as much in music as she is skilful in it. In adornment she is elegant, rather than showy … I am inventing nothing, my dear Sturm; there is no need.' Katherine (Kat) Ashley (née Champernowne) had joined Elizabeth's household in 1536 and had become her governess when Lady Bryan was diverted to the care of young Prince Edward. She was highly regarded by Roger Ascham, and played a part in overseeing Elizabeth's education. Ascham advised her on this responsibility: 'Good Mistress,' he wrote, 'I would have you in any case to labour and not give yourself to ease.' He then cautioned, however: 'the younger, the more tender, the quicker, the easier to break'. But Mrs Ashley and her charge were soon involved in a scandal that brought them both to the edge of breaking-point. It centred upon Thomas Seymour, the Lord Admiral and uncle of Edward VI.

About four months after the King's death in 1547, Katherine Parr had married Thomas Seymour, a man she had loved before marrying Henry. She had regarded her marriage to Henry as a duty; the union with the Lord Admiral was a love-match, at least on Katherine's part. Seymour's first choice as a marriage partner had been Elizabeth, and he discussed this possibility with his brother Edward Seymour – by now 1st Duke of Somerset – another ambitious man who had elevated himself from guardian of the young King to Lord Protector, thus ruling England. Edward Seymour immediately vetoed his brother's plans. However, the subsequent marriage to Katherine brought Thomas into daily contact with Elizabeth, whom he besieged with attention. Thomas Seymour was a tall, handsome man of thirty-eight, and his interest was probably flattering to the fourteen-year-old girl. It was said that she 'did bear some affection' for him, and would blush whenever his name was mentioned. But then, the harmless flirtation grew more dangerous. Seymour would go into Elizabeth's bedchamber early in the morning, dressed only 'in his nightgown' and 'bare-legged'. If she were up, 'he would strike her familiarly on the back and buttocks'. If she were in bed, he would open the bed curtain 'and make as though he would come at her', while she 'would go further into the bed'. One morning, he attempted to kiss Elizabeth in her bed, upon which Mrs Ashley, who slept in Elizabeth's room, 'bade him go away for shame'. Another morning, at Chelsea, Elizabeth heard the privy lock undo, and 'knowing he would come in, ran out of her bed to her maidens'. Kat Ashley remonstrated with Seymour, saying his behaviour was causing slanderous gossip. But he was quite unrepentant. Mrs Ashley then pleaded with Katherine Parr, who regarded the matter as trivial, but who agreed to accompany her husband in future. Thereafter, Katherine joined in the frolic, tickling the girl in bed; on another

Opposite An extract
of the letter Elizabeth
wrote to the Lord
Protector in January
1549, in which she
pleaded her
innocence of any
wrongdoing in
the Thomas
Seymour scandal.
The letter is at
Hatfield House.

occasion, in the garden at Hanworth, Katherine playfully held Elizabeth while Seymour cut the girl's gown into a hundred pieces. However, her tolerance ceased when she unexpectedly found her stepdaughter in Seymour's arms, 'wherefore', according to Thomas Parry, Elizabeth's cofferer (treasurer), she 'fell out with the Lord Admiral and with her Grace also'. If Katherine Parr, who genuinely cared for Elizabeth and her welfare, believed that her stepdaughter was being compromised, she would have ended these playful romps or immediately urged Elizabeth to move to another royal house. Eventually, however, incessant gossip was making the situation alarming, and in the summer of 1548 Elizabeth left Katherine's house – probably at Katherine's suggestion – to spend a few months at Cheshunt, the home of family friend Sir Anthony Denny. From Cheshunt, Elizabeth wrote to her stepmother:

Although I could not be plentiful in giving thanks for the manifold kindness received at your highness's hand at my departure, yet I am something to be born withal for truly I was replete with sorrow to depart from your highness, especially seeing you undoubtful of health, and albeit I answered little I weighed it more deeper when you said you would warn me of all evil that you should hear of me, for if your grace had not a good opinion of me you would not have offered friendship to me that way, that all men judge the contrary, but what may I more say than thank God for providing such friends to me, desiring God to enrich me with their long life.

The correspondence between Elizabeth and her stepmother remained affectionate. Katherine Parr was expecting a child and Elizabeth in one of her letters wished her 'a most lucky deliverance'. However, six weeks later, while giving birth to a daughter, Katherine died at Sudeley Castle.

After Katherine's death, it was widely rumoured that Thomas Seymour would resume his intention to marry Elizabeth. When the gossip reached Elizabeth she played the matter down, saying it was but 'London news'. Still, the rumours persisted and grew increasingly dangerous, for Seymour's plans encompassed other royal children, too. After his wife's death, he continued to maintain Katherine's household of ladies, including Elizabeth's cousin Lady Jane Grey, who remained under his care at Sudeley Castle. It was Thomas Seymour's scheme to marry her to the young King Edward as part of an intrigue to supplant his brother Edward, the Lord Protector. The final blow fell when the Lord Admiral and his co-conspirators were discovered in an antechamber of King Edward's bedroom. Their plans to abduct the King were only prevented by the barking of the boy's spaniel, which alerted the guard. Thomas Seymour

for I knowe I haue a soule to saue as wele as other fokes haue wherfore
I wil aboue al thinge haue respect vnto this same . Off ther be any more
thinges wche I can remembre I wil ether write it mi selfe or cause maister
Tirwit to write it . Maister Tirwit and others haue tolde me that ther go-
eth rumor abrode wche be greatly bothe agenste myne honor, and honest,
wche aboue al other thinkes I esteme, wche be these, that I shuide am in the
tower and with childe by my Lord Admiral, My Lord these ar shameful
chandlers, for the wche besides the great desier I haue to se the Kinges Maie-
I shal most hartely desire your Lordship that I may come to the court after your
first determination, that I may shewe my selfe there as I am . Writen in hast frome Affelde
his 28 of Ianuarye .

Your assured frende to my litel power .

Elizabeth

was arrested on 17 January 1549 and charged on several counts of high treason, one of which was his scheming to marry Elizabeth without the permission of the Lord Protector, the Privy Council or the King. In accordance with Henry VIII's will, the claim of Elizabeth or Mary to the throne would be cancelled should either, during King Edward's lifetime, marry without the consent of the Council. By inference, any man who attempted to marry either claimant without the necessary permission involved both himself and the girl in serious charges. Elizabeth's flirtation with Seymour now entangled her in a perilous situation. Thomas Parry and Kat Ashley were taken to the Tower of London for questioning; Elizabeth cried at their arrest. Sir Robert Tyrwhitt, a shrewd investigator, was sent by the Council to interrogate Elizabeth, by now at Hatfield. Tyrwhitt tried relentlessly to pressure her into a confession of guilt with the complicity of Ashley and Parry. 'But', he reported to the Council, 'she will not confess any practice by Mrs Ashley or the cofferer.' He soon became exasperated with Elizabeth's resolve: 'She hath a very good wit and nothing is got out of her but by great policy.' Elizabeth wrote to the Lord Protector, pleading her innocence and pointing out that Kat Ashley had never advised her to marry, and that 'always when any talked of marriage that she would never have me marry, neither in England nor out of England without the consent of the king's majesty, your grace's and the council's'. In the same letter, Elizabeth wrote of disturbing rumours being spread about:

... which be greatly both against my honour and honesty, which above all other things I esteem, which be these; that I am in the tower; and with child by my Lord Admiral. My Lord, these are shameful slanders for the which besides the great desire I have to see the King's Majesty, I shall most heartily desire your Lordship that I may come to the court after your first determination, that I may show myself there as I am.

She signed her letter: 'Your assured friend to my litel power, Elizabeth.'

Opposite A window looking onto the privy garden at Hatfield (today known as the 'Old Palace'), where Elizabeth stayed during the Thomas Seymour scandal.

Tyrwhitt continued his endless questioning, but made no further progress. 'I do verily believe', he wrote to the Council, 'that there hath been some secret promise between My Lady, Mistress Ashley, and the Cofferer, never to confess to death.' However, a week after Elizabeth wrote to the Lord Protector, Kat Ashley was examined and probably suffered either the threat or the reality of torture, for she signed a confession in which the buttocks-slapping, early morning romps and other incidents were revealed. A copy of the confession was sent to Hatfield and shown to Elizabeth who was 'much abashed and half breathless' when she read it. But even then, Tyrwhitt could not get the girl to admit to a definite plot. The Lord Protector then wrote to Elizabeth urging her to comply. She responded: 'Whereas your Grace doth will me to credit Master Tyrwhitt, I have done so, and will do so as long as he willeth me (as he doth not) to nothing but to that which is for mine honour and mine honesty.' The Council then sent Tyrwhitt's wife to Hatfield to take Mrs Ashley's place as governess, causing Elizabeth so much distress that she wept through the night and 'lowered all day'; she would have no mistress but Mistress Ashley. She wrote again to the Lord Protector, this time explaining her objections to Lady Tyrwhitt: 'the people will say that I deserved through my lewd demeanour to have such a one … And seeing they make so evil reports already [there would now be] an increasing of their evil tongues.' The Lord Protector had previously told Elizabeth that anyone who slandered her would be punished. But, being ever mindful of public opinion herself, Elizabeth would not report the names of those who were gossiping about her for she feared that it would lead to 'a breeding of an evil name of me, that I am glad to punish them, and so get the evil will of the people, which thing I would be loth to have'. As an alternative, she suggested that the Lord Protector together with the Privy Council 'send forth a proclamation into the counties that they restrain their tongues declaring how the tales are but lies, it should make both the people think that you and the council have great regard that no such rumours should be spread of any of the King's Majesty's Sisters …'.

Elizabeth continued under the supervision of Lady Tyrwhitt, and a few weeks after her last letter to Edward Seymour, she wrote again, pleading for the reinstatement of Mrs Ashley for three reasons:

First because that she hath been with me a long time, and many years and hath taken great labour and pain in bringing of me up in learning and honesty.… The second is because I think

that whatsoever she hath done in my Lord Admiral's matter as concerning the marriage of me, she did it because, knowing him to be one of the council, she thought he would not go about any such thing without he had the council's consent. The third cause is because that it shall, and doth, make men think that I am not clear of the deed myself, but that it is pardoned in me because of my youth, because that she I loved well is in such a place, and I have at this time gone forth with it. Which I pray God be taken no other ways than it is meant.

In the same letter, she mentions the proclamation sought in her previous correspondence, and it seems that she had been told that it was sent out as requested. There is, however, no record of this proclamation ever being made. A month after his arrest, the case against Thomas Seymour came to a close, and he was executed on 20 March 1549. Mrs Ashley and Thomas Parry returned to Elizabeth's household.

After Thomas Seymour's death, and during the remaining four years of King Edward's reign, Elizabeth threw herself into her studies, gaining a reputation as one of the most accomplished and learned young ladies in the realm. She was 'inflamed with zeal for the religion of Christ', wrote John Hooper, Bishop of Gloucester and Worcester, in 1550. 'She not only knows what true religion is, but has acquired such proficiency in Greek and Latin that she is able to defend it by the most just arguments.' It seems that she also adopted a somewhat scholarly appearance, leaving off the rich fabrics, gold and jewels that later would become such an essential part of her attire. Her beautiful and learned cousin Lady Jane Grey, though four years younger than Elizabeth, was more fashionable in her choice of dress and accessories. The contrast between the two girls was noticed. In 1551, Lady Jane's tutor John Aylmer, Bishop of London, wrote to the Protestant reformer John Bullinger – with whom Jane, a fervent Protestant, probably corresponded through Aylmer – begging him to admonish his pupil 'as to what embellishment and adornment of person is becoming in young women professing godliness'. Aylmer suggested that Bullinger advise Lady Jane to emulate Elizabeth 'who goes clad in every respect as becomes a young maiden'. 'And yet', he added, 'no one is induced by the example of so illustrious a lady, and in so much gospel light, to lay aside, much less look down upon, gold, jewels and braidings of the hair.' Elizabeth's favourite colours in clothing were black and white, said to have magical powers. King Edward called her his 'sweet Sister Temperance'.

A chamber at
Hatfield, the
Hertfordshire country
manor which had
been the residence of
the bishops of Ely
before Henry VIII
acquired it in 1538.
Elizabeth cherished
the palace as a
comfortable refuge
until she ascended the
throne in 1558 at the
age of twenty-five.

During the Seymour scandal, King Edward would not allow Elizabeth to come to Court; she had been absent for eighteen months. Such a ban from Edward was painful for Elizabeth, who was always eager to appear at Court with all the decorum due a daughter of Henry VIII. However, when Elizabeth's disgrace began to be forgotten, Edward invited her to join him for the Christmas festivities of 1549. An ambassador to the Court reported that: 'She was received with great pomp and triumph and is continually with the King'. A year later, the 'sister to the King came to London with a great suite of gentlemen and ladies, escorted by 100 of the King's horse. She was most honourably received by the Council.' The ambassador believed the Privy Council's respectful reception of Elizabeth was 'to show the people how much glory belongs to her who has embraced the new religion and is become a very great lady'.

In 1550, Elizabeth secured Durham Place, a London property left to her together with other lands in her father's will: it had taken four years to settle her ownership with the Council. The mansion was ideally located, stretching along a curve in the Thames between her half-brother's London palace at Whitehall – then England's seat of power – and Somerset House, the home of the Lord Protector, Edward Seymour, 1st Duke of Somerset, until his death by execution in 1552. Durham Place, once used by Anne Boleyn, was large and commodious, with well-manicured gardens running down to the river. Elizabeth also exchanged some lands in Lincolnshire to possess Hatfield, the Hertfordshire house she had loved since childhood. Built between 1479 and 1483, Hatfield had once been the palace of the bishops of Ely; it had been acquired by Henry VIII in 1538. The manor house was constructed of russet brick in the form of a quadrangle. On one side of the quadrangle was the great hall, surmounted by a tower with private chambers and state apartments overlooking the gardens and orchard. Opposite were the gatehouse and guardroom, and on either side, additional lodgings and domestic offices. In preparation for the arrival of young Prince Edward in 1543, alterations had been made to the kitchen and sculleries, and a fishpond was dug near the bakehouse. There had also been payments for mowing the orchard, tidying the alleys and pruning the trees. Hatfield was set in a great park of several hundred acres containing 'venerable oaks' and beeches, and was well stocked with deer and other game. During her reign, Elizabeth would add a new window to the presence chamber and stairs descending to the orchard at Hatfield. Thus, at the age of just sixteen and a half years, Elizabeth was the owner of a country

manor and a prime London mansion. By this time, her household had
increased to 120 persons.

In March 1551, John Dudley, Earl of Warwick (who was soon to become
Duke of Northumberland), began negotiations to marry Elizabeth to the brother
of the Duke of Guise. Marriages were also considered to the son of the Duke of
Florence (who was only eleven years old); the second son of the Duke of
Saxony; the son of the Duke of Ferrara; and Francesco d' Este, the brother of
the Duke of Ferrara. But the Guise connection was the most attractive as a
means of strengthening the alliance with France. In 1551, King Edward
entertained Mary of Guise, the Dowager of Scotland, at Hampton Court.
It was the first time he had entertained another sovereign, and the Court was
intoxicated with excitement. According to John Aylmer, the ladies 'frownsed
and curled and double curled' their hair. But Elizabeth pointedly affected a
simple style, abstaining from both make-up and finery, and 'kepte hir olde
mayderly shamefastnesse'; the other ladies were 'dressed and paynted like
pecockes'. Nor did she wear any jewels: Aylmer said that for seven years Lady
Elizabeth avoided wearing the jewels left to her in her father's will, and 'there
came never gold nor stone upon her head tyl her sister enforced her to lay her
former sobrenes and bear her company in her glistering gaynes'. Lady Elizabeth
also continued in her maidenly state with regard to marriage. The various
marriage negotiations came to nothing. Yet another hopeful, the Earl of
Pembroke, tried 'to obtain her in marriage, but she refuse[d] her consent'.

After the downfall and execution of Edward Seymour in 1552, John Dudley,
by now Duke of Northumberland, assumed the role, but not the title, of Lord
Protector, becoming the most powerful man in England. As such, he was in a
position to comply with Elizabeth's request for the use of Somerset House in
exchange for Durham Place, which she had never occupied. Somerset House,
with its innovative use of classical order, was one of the most important houses
of the Tudor period. It was begun in 1547 as a typical early sixteenth-century
courtyard house laid out between a main London city street and the River
Thames. The distinguishing feature was its street façade, which had an entrance
designed like a classical triumphal arch framed by Doric columns and
surmounted by two storeys of windows united by pilasters beneath a flat roof.
Flanking the east and west ends of the house were bays with two stages of paired
windows framed by Doric and Ionic columns or pilasters beneath pediments. It
was unlike anything England had seen before, and surpassed even France and

Right Elizabeth liked
to walk in the great
oak wood
surrounding Hatfield.
The park was well
stocked with various
game so that Elizabeth
could enjoy another
of her favourite
activities, hunting.

Opposite A view
of Hatfield showing
an entrance to the
great hall. This side
of the russet-brick
building overlooked
the gardens.

the Low Countries in understanding the Renaissance lessons of classical order. The construction of the house had been supervised by Lord Protector Somerset's steward John Thynne, who went on to build Longleat in Wiltshire. Somerset House was built with knowledge and intelligence: a fitting abode for 'Sister Temperance'. Another member of the Lord Protector's household, William Cecil, later Lord Burghley, used his familiarity with Somerset House when constructing Burghley House in Lincolnshire; he later became Elizabeth's Principal Secretary of State.

In the spring of 1553, the fifteen-year-old King was dying of tuberculosis. During the latter stages of his illness, Elizabeth had attempted to visit him. She set out from Hatfield but turned back after receiving a message presumably instructing her not to come. She later wrote to him of her disappointment: 'Like a shipman in stormy weather plucks down the sails tarrying for better wind, so did I, most noble King, in my unfortunate chance a Thursday pluck down the high sails of my joy and comfort and do trust one day that as troublesome waves have repulsed me backward, so a gentle wind will bring me forward to my haven.' She had earlier given Edward a present of her translation of Bernardino Ochino's 'Sermon XII' from his *Prediche*. In the accompanying letter, she wrote: 'no one can match the extent of my love and good feeling towards you … you are my only and most dearly beloved brother.'

Edward died on 6 July 1553. Before his death he had drawn up a document, 'My Device for the Succession', bequeathing the Crown to Lady Jane Grey and her male heirs. His fear of Mary's Catholic religion and its re-establishment in England was so great that he excluded Mary from the throne. Elizabeth was also excluded because, he claimed, she was only 'of the half blood', though under Henry's will, which was legally sanctioned, Mary was to ascend the throne, and Elizabeth was second in line. Three days later, on 9 July, Lady Jane was proclaimed queen. Town criers were ordered to shout from every street corner in London that Mary and Elizabeth were bastards. Mary retreated to the well-fortified castle of Framlingham in East Anglia, where she mustered forces; Elizabeth remained at Hatfield. For nine days, the country was in turmoil until on 19 July the Privy Council declared their allegiance to Mary; later that day she was proclaimed Queen Mary I in London.

Elizabeth immediately wrote to congratulate her half-sister. She also asked, in her letter, what she should wear – mourning for the half-brother she loved, or something more festive to celebrate her sister's victory? Even then she

During his lifetime, he made drawings and plans of well-known buildings of the day. His collection of drawings is now considered the most important documentary record of Elizabethan architecture.

weighed the mood of the Court and the mood of the country in order to present the best possible public image.

By this time, she was ordering her clothes from France and could choose among a selection of stylish gowns. On 29 July, diarist Henry Machyn recorded that 'came riding through London my Lady Elizabeth's Grace and through Fleet Street, and so to my Lord of Somerset's place that was, and it is now my Lady Grace's, attended with 2,000 horse with spears and bows and guns'. Four days later, Elizabeth, followed by a thousand horsemen, rode out of London to meet Mary at Wanstead; disappointingly, there is no record of what she wore.

At the coronation, Elizabeth, dressed in a robe of crimson velvet trimmed with ermine, carried her half-sister's train. It was probably the last happy day she would know throughout the five years of Mary's reign. In the new queen's first parliament, Catherine of Aragon's marriage to Henry was declared lawful, but Elizabeth, however, remained illegitimate. The Catholic zealot Stephen Gardiner, Mary's Lord Chancellor, who had once been hostile to Catherine of Aragon, and had carried the robes of Anne Boleyn at her coronation, now spoke publicly against Elizabeth's legitimacy. At Court, Henry's nieces Lady Margaret Douglas, Countess of Lennox, and Frances Brandon, Duchess of Suffolk, were given precedence over Elizabeth. In addition to these humiliations, she was spied upon: Mary had reinstated the Catholic religion, and Elizabeth, being a Protestant, was a likely figurehead for anti-Catholic rebels. The Queen expected her half-sister to set an example by attending Mass and embracing what was, after all, the state religion. At first Elizabeth was reluctant, and reputedly wore at her waist a little gold book in which was transcribed 'The Prayer of King Edward VI'. Mary gave her a present of a rosary made from red and white coral, but at the same time she began to show open dislike for Elizabeth, saying that she would become like her mother, a woman 'who had caused great trouble in the Kingdom'. The Queen's dislike was further inflamed by her advisors. Elizabeth realized that the situation was getting dangerous, and decided to appear to conform by attending Mass. But the strain was becoming intolerable. Many Protestants were going into exile, among them Lady Katherine Knollys, daughter of Anne Boleyn's sister Mary. Elizabeth wrote to her cousin wishing her well: '… time and distance of place, separates not the love of friends, nor deprives not the show of good will…. My power but small, my love as great as them whose gifts may tell their friendship's tale.' She signed her letter 'Cor Rotto' ('Broken Heart'). A short while later, Elizabeth asked for,

Above A sixteenth-century girdle book. Fashionable ladies of the Tudor period wore miniature prayer books encased in sumptuous bindings, dangling like pomanders from jewelled chains encircling the waist. Elizabeth sometimes wore such a book, both before and after becoming queen.

and was granted, permission to go to Ashridge. Before leaving the Court, she begged Mary not to believe any accusations that might be made against her without first allowing her the opportunity to clear herself. As a parting gift, Mary gave her half-sister a sable hood for warmth against the December frost. Immediately upon arriving at Ashridge, Elizabeth dutifully wrote to Mary requesting copes and chasubles for the Catholic priests who had accompanied her to Hertfordshire. She wrote again in January 1554 to congratulate Mary on completing her marriage negotiations.

Some weeks before Elizabeth's departure for Ashridge, Mary had decided to marry King Philip II of Spain. Her choice was widely unpopular, provoking English xenophobia in general, and fear of Spanish domination in particular. The inevitable conspiracy against the Crown occurred on 25 January 1554, when Sir Thomas Wyatt of Kent, with several thousand men in arms, marched towards London. As part of the conspiracy, sectional uprisings were simultaneously planned in Devon, Suffolk, Herefordshire and Leicestershire, with anticipated naval and financial support from France. But these uprisings failed. The rebellion collapsed and Wyatt was captured on 7 February. Amongst Wyatt's conspirators was Edward Courtenay, Earl of Devon, and great-great grandson of Edward IV. Courtenay, a Catholic, had been imprisoned in the Tower of London by Henry VIII in 1538, when he was only twelve years old, because his claim to the throne was stronger than Henry's own; Mary had him released. The conspirators had intended to bring about a marriage between Elizabeth and Courtenay, followed by their joint succession to the throne. When this was revealed, Courtenay was also arrested, and Elizabeth summoned from Ashridge. Elizabeth was ill at the time, and her doctors told the Queen that she could not be moved. But Mary considered it a deceit, Elizabeth feigning illness to gain sympathy. She commanded that her half-sister be brought to London in a litter. Elizabeth and her entourage travelled in slow stages, taking five days to make a thirty-five-mile journey normally accomplished in three. They arrived in London on 23 February and were met and escorted by the Queen's Guard. Elizabeth halted the procession and had the curtains of her litter pulled back, so that onlookers might observe, and perhaps be moved by, her appearance. She lay weak, propped against pillows, her pale complexion made more so against her white gown.

Wyatt and other leaders of the conspiracy were kept alive until April in the hope that under interrogation and torture they would implicate Elizabeth. It was discovered that Wyatt had written to Elizabeth at Ashridge, but had received no written replies. 'As for the traitor Wyatt', Elizabeth responded, when she herself was questioned, 'he might peradventure write to me a letter, but on my faith I never received any from him'. From the scaffold, Wyatt declared that neither Elizabeth nor Courtenay had any prior knowledge of his conspiracy. Courtenay was released, but Elizabeth remained under guard. She was first held at St James's Palace and then, ominously, moved to the Tower. Before being taken there, she asked for pen and paper to write to Mary. She was convinced that her life depended upon an interview with her sister. She feared the power of the privy councillors and recalled that the Lord Protector had once mentioned that his brother Thomas Seymour would never have been executed had they met before the trial. While Elizabeth wrote to the Queen pleading innocence and begging for an interview, the tide of the Thames rose, making London Bridge impassable by barge. The move to the Tower had to be delayed until the following day, Palm Sunday. Across the bottom half of her letter, Elizabeth drew diagonal lines so that no one could forge a postscript. Below these lines, she added: 'I humbly crave but only one word of answer from yourself.'

She entered the Tower, 'a place more wonted for a false traitor than a true subject', through the Water Gate, accompanied by her six ladies-in-waiting, a gentleman usher and another gentleman. 'Oh Lord!', she declared, 'I never thought to have come here as a prisoner; and I pray you all good friends and fellows, bear me witness that I come in no traitor, but as a true woman to the Queen's Majesty as any is now living, and thereon will take my death.' According to tradition, she made this speech from the mooring at the entrance to the Tower. In the previous month, Jane Grey had been beheaded at the Tower, as had her husband Guildford Dudley, son of John Dudley, Duke of Northumberland. Years earlier, Elizabeth's mother and her cousin Katherine Howard had both been beheaded there. For Elizabeth, the Tower would always be associated with doom. Anticipating that her own head would soon be on the block, she requested a swordsman as executioner. The sword was preferred to the axe, her mother had made a similar arrangement.

The warders of the Tower were lined up inside the Water Gate. As Lady Elizabeth approached, some of them broke ranks and knelt down shouting: 'God preserve your Grace!' She, together with her ladies, was imprisoned on the first floor of the Bell Tower, in a stone chamber with three arched windows and stone window seats. She was allowed to take exercise on the 'leads', a

narrow passageway between the Bell Tower and Beauchamp Tower. An argument arose concerning her diet, since it was thought unseemly for an heiress to the throne to eat the common food of other prisoners. In the end, she was allowed to dine more in accordance with her status, with the attendance of two yeomen of her chamber, one of her robes, two of her pantry and ewry (a room for storing ewers of water and other liquids), one of her buttery, one of her cellar, another of her larder and two of her kitchen. However, the Lord Chamberlain had to escort them, and the provisions were searched before they could be served to Elizabeth. She remained in the Tower for two months. In John Foxe's *Book of Martyrs*, a tale is related of a little four-year-old boy, the son of one of the warders, who brought Elizabeth flowers during her walks until he was observed and threatened with a beating. It was thought he might be concealing messages hidden in the bouquet. 'Mistress,' the child called to her through the grille, 'I may bring you no more flowers.'

Elizabeth, though considered by Mary and the Council to be a 'heretic' and a threat to the Crown, was very popular with the people. She was young, beautiful, charming and a Protestant, and, with her red-gold hair, she resembled her father. It was thought that because of her popularity, Elizabeth could neither be put to death nor ousted from the succession without causing more riots and rebellion. For the same reasons, she could not continue to be kept in the Tower. It was, nevertheless, also dangerous to set her free. To have her at Court would have offended Mary's dignity, so it was decided to keep her in close captivity at the royal manor of Woodstock in Oxfordshire. She was taken first by barge to Richmond Palace. At Richmond, she was watched all night by soldiers and denied access to even her most private attendants, causing her to be convinced that orders had been given to put her secretly to death. The next day, she was moved on to Windsor Castle, where she was locked not in the castle itself but in the Dean's house near St George's Chapel. She was then taken to West Wycombe and thereafter to Thame in Oxfordshire, where she 'was verie princelie entertained' by Lord Williams, High Sheriff of the County. Elizabeth arrived at Woodstock on 23 May 1554. All along the route, villagers and farmhands had cheered as she passed. The church bells of Aston had rung out; at Wheatley and Stanton St John, people had cried 'God save your Grace!'; at Rycote, housewives had tossed cakes and biscuits into Elizabeth's litter until it became so heavy with their presents that she had to beg them to stop. It was clear that precautions were necessary at Woodstock to prevent a rescue. Sir

Henry Bedingfield had been appointed Elizabeth's 'jaylor', though on his knees he pleaded that she regard him as her 'officer'. 'From such officers,' she said, 'good Lord deliver me.' She was lodged ignominiously in the gatehouse of the palace, in a chamber with an 'arched roof of Irish oak, curiously carved, painted blue sprinkled with gold'. She was not allowed to walk in the garden without Sir Henry, 'nor was she to receive any message, letter or token to or from any manner of person'. She did write to Mary, but her letter was not well received, provoking a royal censure: 'Our pleasure is that we shall not hereafter be molested any more with her disguised and colourable letters.' Her books were also restricted. She had arrived at Woodstock with a prayer book from Henry VIII's reign, and soon after asked for an English translation of the Bible, although under Mary it had become illegal to read the Bible in English. Her cofferer, Thomas Parry, brought her Cicero and the Psalms in Latin; these she was allowed to keep after Bedingfield cleared them with the Council. And so it went on for nearly a year: Elizabeth would put a request to Bedingfield, he in turn would canvas the Council, and the request would then be granted or denied – more often the latter. Books, paper and ink were restricted, but it seems that needle and thread were not, for Elizabeth stitched a cushion with gold and silver embroidery. She fell ill with an old complaint – swelling in her face and body – and asked that the Queen's physicians be sent. They were unavailable, so others were offered. These Elizabeth refused. 'I am not minded', she exclaimed, 'to make any stranger privy to the state of my body, but commit it to God'. The royal physicians were eventually sent to her. At some point during her incarceration at Woodstock, she used a diamond to scratch a few words into a window pane:

Much suspected by me,

Nothing proved can be, quoth Elizabeth prisoner.

With a piece of charcoal she supposedly wrote upon a window-shutter:

O Fortune! how thy reckless wavering state,

Hath fraught with cares my troubled wit!

Witness this present Prison whither fate

Hath borne me, and the joys I quit.

Thou causedest the guilty to be loosed

From bands, wherewith are Innocents inclosed;

Opposite The narrow passageway at the Tower of London known as the 'leads', on which Elizabeth was allowed to exercise during her imprisonment there in 1554. From here, Elizabeth would have had a view overlooking the River Thames and the city. From her quarters in the Bell Tower, she would have seen the place of execution on Tower Hill.

Above The *Epistles of St Paul*, which belonged to Elizabeth. It has long been held that she consoled herself with this book during her period of imprisonment at Woodstock. This is unlikely, however, since this English edition of the book was not printed until 1576. The cover, which Elizabeth embroidered with silver and gold thread, shows a heart with a flower growing through it.

Causing the guiltless to be straight reserved,
And freeing those that death had well deserved;
But by her envy can be nothing wrought,
So God send to my Foes all they have thought.

Elizabeth, Prisoner.

While Elizabeth was at Woodstock, Mary and King Philip were married. A few months after the wedding, the Queen believed herself pregnant, and on 27 November 1554 the news was proclaimed throughout London. Mary ordered Elizabeth's release from Woodstock on 17 April 1555, and she was transferred to Hampton Court. She was kept in seclusion until Philip intervened and Elizabeth was allowed an interview with the Queen; without a reconciliation with Mary, Elizabeth could never have hoped to become the future queen. 'You stiffly still persevere in your truth', said Mary angrily. 'Belike you will not confess, but that you have been wrongfully punished.' 'I must not say so, if it please your Majesty, to you', replied Elizabeth, 'I have borne the burden and must bear it. I humbly beseech your Majesty to have a good opinion of me.'

By the end of April 1555, it was rumoured that Queen Mary had given birth to a son. Elizabeth stitched her a full set of baby clothes of fine white linen decorated with red embroidery, which she had probably begun making while still imprisoned in Woodstock. But the birth was an illusion, and a baby never arrived: the much-celebrated pregnancy had been a false one. Mary's health now began the decline that would eventually lead to her death three and a half years later.

The following August, the Court moved to Oatlands, a great country house in Surrey acquired and enlarged by Henry VIII. The purpose of the move was to allow Mary a gradual re-emergence into public life, attained with the least embarrassment. The Court later went on to Greenwich Palace, while Philip returned to Spain; indeed, he made only two brief visits to England throughout his wife's reign. While Elizabeth was with Mary at Greenwich, she attended Mass and outwardly appeared to have accepted the Catholic faith. The courtiers were kinder towards her, and in some ways Elizabeth's position was becoming more secure, but there was the ever-present fear that she would be dragged into plots. Mary had begun a campaign of religious persecutions during which hundreds of 'heretics' were burnt at the stake, including Elizabeth's godfather Archbishop Cranmer. The mood of the country was turning against the Queen.

Sweet Sister Temperance

Opposite An extract
of the inscription
found inside
Elizabeth's copy of
the *Epistles of St Paul*,
and thought to be in
her own hand. The
inscription supports
the belief that she
had the book at
Woodstock, for during
her imprisonment she
would have sought
solace in 'the pleasant
fields of the holy
scriptures', thereby
hoping that she would
'less perceive the
bitterness of [her]
miserable life'.

Below An astrolabe
made for Elizabeth in
1559 by the Flemish
instrument maker
Thomas Gemini. She
had a number of
astrolabes made for
her during her
lifetime

In October 1555, Mary moved to St James's Palace to be in London for the meeting of Parliament. Elizabeth was given permission to return to Hatfield; she had not seen her beloved manor house for nearly two years. As soon as she was settled, she sent for Roger Ascham, and tutor and student once again resumed their daily readings of Latin and Greek. But even in the Hertfordshire countryside, Elizabeth was never far removed from intrigue. One of her servants had been sent to the Tower for seditious words, another soon followed. Dr John Dee, astrologer to both Mary and Elizabeth, was also arrested. His crime was probably to show the Queen's horoscope to her half-sister, pointing out the contrasting planetary aspects in the two maps, tantamount at that time to treason. He was sent to the Tower more than once, but always obtained his freedom. John Dee was not only an astrologer and astronomer, he was also a mathematician, alchemist and scholar, a friend of both John Cheke's and Roger Ascham's. In Elizabeth's reign, he became a foreign spy, reporting, in code, to both the Queen and William Cecil on intrigues abroad. His coded letters were signed using the numerals '007'. During Mary's reign, Elizabeth and Dee corresponded through his cousin, Thomas Parry's sister Blanche Parry, who was a maid of honour to Elizabeth and her close friend. Dee encouraged Elizabeth's interest in astrology and clairvoyance, and he made an astrolabe for her. He was always concerned about Elizabeth's welfare, advising her on herbs, medicines and diet. It seems that he had a premonition she would never marry. Elizabeth's Italian tutor was also arrested on a charge of sedition, set free, and then rearrested. On his second arrest, Kat Ashley was taken to the Tower with him: a great coffer full of anti-Catholic books and ballads, and other seditious papers had been found in her chamber. Mary wrote a kindly letter to Elizabeth full of goodwill, inviting her to return to Court. She also included a valuable ring. Elizabeth accepted the gift but declined the invitation. The point was understood, however: Elizabeth was not suspected of complicity in the crimes of her staff. Nevertheless, in June 1556 Sir Thomas Pope was sent to Hatfield as her custodian, 'in ward and custody though in such decorous and honorable form'. Elizabeth was quite happy with Sir Thomas. They talked together of his plans for Trinity College, Oxford, of which he was both founder and benefactor. 'She often asketh

me about the course I have devised for my scholars', he wrote, 'and that part of my statutes respecting study I have shown her, which she likes well.' It seems that Sir Thomas was equally pleased with his ward, for during Shrovetide (the three days before Ash Wednesday) he 'made for the Lady Elizabeth, all at his own cost, a great and rich masquing in the great hall at Hatfield'. There were twelve minstrels 'antickly disguised' with 'forty-six or more gentlemen and ladies, many of them knights or nobles, or ladies of honour apparelled in crimson satin, embroidered with wreaths of gold, and garnished with borders of hanging pearl … and [there was] a device of a castle of cloth of gold, set with pomegranates about the battlements with shields of knights hanging therefrom, and six knights in rich harness turneyed [jousted]'. During the evening in the hall, the company enjoyed a banquet of seventy dishes, and 'after, a voidee of spices and subtleties, with 30 plates'. The court cupboard, or buffet, in the hall was furnished '12 stages high with vessels of gold and silver'. The next day, the ladies and gentlemen were entertained with a performance of *Holofernes*, a play based on the popular biblical story. This was perhaps not the best political choice at the time, considering the unpopularity of the Queen's marriage to the Spanish king. In the play, the heroine Judith, in order to deliver her people from the onslaught of Holofernes, general of the Assyrian king, enters her enemy's camp, and, while he is in a drunken state, cuts off his head. Judith then shows Holofernes's head to her people, giving them the courage to rush upon the invading army and win the battle. Soon after the Shrovetide entertainments, Queen Mary wrote to Sir Thomas indicating that she 'misliked these fooleries', and so they ceased.

In August 1556, an impostor named Cleobury declared himself to be Lord Courtenay, and at Yaxley in Sussex proclaimed Elizabeth queen, and himself – 'her beloved bedfellow' – king. When Elizabeth heard of the mischief she was greatly distressed, and wrote a long letter to Mary agonizing over the discredit to her name and character, and asserting her innocence. In the letter, she wished

Above The great hall at Hatfield Old Palace, where Sir Thomas Pope organized a Shrovetide banquet and entertainments for Elizabeth in 1557. The following year, in November 1558, the newly proclaimed Queen Elizabeth held her first meeting of the Privy Council here.

Sweet Sister Temperance

there were 'good surgeons for making anatomies of hearts that might show my thoughts to your Majesty', the thoughts of a faithful subject. The real Lord Courtenay died under mysterious circumstances some weeks later, and the matter was conveniently resolved.

By the spring of 1557, the two half-sisters appeared to have become happier together, more like they had been on the day Mary, with Elizabeth behind her, rode into London to claim the throne. Elizabeth visited Mary at Whitehall Palace and at Richmond Palace, and in April she was escorted from Hatfield to Enfield by a 'retinue of twelve ladies clothed in white satin on ambling palfries', and twenty yeomen in green, all on horseback, so that 'Her Grace might hunt the hart'. At the chase, Elizabeth was met by fifty archers in scarlet boots and yellow caps armed with gilded bows. One of them presented her with a silver-headed arrow winged with peacock's feathers. She was later given a knife and 'gratified' with the honour of cutting a buck's throat. In the same month, Mary visited her half-sister at Hatfield. On the morning after her arrival, and after Mass, the Queen and Lady Elizabeth 'were treated to a grand exhibition of bear-baiting, with which their Highnesses were right well entertained'. Dinner was served in the great hall, which had been adorned for the Queen's reception with a sumptuous suite of tapestry called 'The Hangings of the Siege of Antioch'. That night, a play was presented by a company of singers attached to St Paul's Cathedral. After the play, one of the singers, a boy named Maximilian Poynes, who had an exquisite voice, sang while Elizabeth accompanied on the virginals.

Meanwhile, everything Mary and Elizabeth did together or separately – every look, gesture and tone of voice – was observed by ambassadors to the Court, professional tattlers. In the spring of 1557, Giovanni Michiel, the Venetian ambassador, wrote to the Doge reporting on twenty-three-year-old Elizabeth. Michiel's views reveal her confidence as Henry's daughter and rightful heir to the Tudor dynasty. They also acknowledge her power, even before succeeding to the throne, to evoke love and support, and to use femininity as a political tool. Queen Mary, Michiel asserted, regarded Elizabeth as 'the illegitimate child of a criminal, who was punished as a public strumpet'. He allowed himself to be impressed with Elizabeth's command of Italian, but he found her:

Proud and haughty, as although she knows she was born of such a mother, she nevertheless does not consider herself of inferior degree to the Queen, whom she equals in self-esteem; nor

Opposite A hand-
coloured genealogical
chart tracing
Elizabeth's ancestry
all the way back to
Adam. Such charts
were commonly used
to 'prove' a monarch's
superior pedigree and
therefore legitimize
their right to rule.
The chart is at
Hatfield House.

does she believe herself less legitimate than her Majesty, alleging in her own favour that her mother would never cohabit with the King unless by way of marriage, with the authority of the Church…. She prides herself on her father and glories in him; everybody saying that she also resembles him more than the Queen does and he therefore always liked her and had her brought up in the same way as the Queen.

He goes on to mention Elizabeth's financial struggles:

She now lives upon [the] settlement from her father, but is always in debt, and would be much more so did she not steadily restrain herself to avoid any increase of the Queen's hatred and anger, either by increasing the number of gentlemen servants of her household, or by adding to her expenditure in any other way; and here I may add that there is not a lord or gentleman in the kingdom who has failed, and continues endeavouring, to enter her service himself or to place one of his sons or brothers in it, such being the love and affection borne her.

Her poverty stirred 'tacit compassion … as it seems strange and vexatious to everybody that being the daughter of a king she should be treated and acknowledged so sparingly'. Michiel then claimed that Elizabeth, at the time of Mary's pregnancy, had worked to gain the sympathies of the Spanish members of the Court, particularly Philip: she 'contrived to ingratiate herself with all the Spaniards and especially with the King, that ever since no one has favoured her more than he does'.

Whatever Philip's feelings for Elizabeth, they did not inhibit his pursuit of a marriage between his sister-in-law and Emmanuel Philibert, later Duke of Savoy. He was anxious to cement a Tudor–Habsburg alliance. In this effort there had been previous proposals to marry Elizabeth to Archduke Ferdinand, the son of Charles V's brother the King of the Romans, and even to Philip's eleven-year-old son Don Carlos. Spain had been drawn into war with France by Pope Paul IV's decision to expel Habsburg armies from Italy. Although Philip's marriage contract with Mary precluded England from becoming engaged in a war which Spain might be fighting against her hereditary enemies, a marriage between Elizabeth and the Duke of Savoy would certainly have been useful to the Spanish king. He urged Mary (who was always eager to please her husband) to persuade Elizabeth of the importance of the match, and when this failed he enlisted the aid of his cousins the duchesses of Parma and Lorraine, inviting them to England to meet Elizabeth and to convince her of the Duke's attractions. But a month later, they left England without achieving their objective. There was yet another contender in the wings. The father of Prince Erik of Sweden had ambitions to secure a marriage between Elizabeth and his son, and sent his ambassador to England to make the proposal. But being either in a hurry or ignorant of English protocol, the ambassador bypassed the Queen and the Privy Council, and went directly to Hatfield where he made the proposal by proxy to Elizabeth herself. Elizabeth immediately informed the Queen, who urgently dispatched Sir Thomas Pope to Hatfield to ascertain Elizabeth's preference: the Duke of Savoy or Prince Erik of Sweden? Sir Thomas wrote to the Queen with an account of the interview. Elizabeth asked him to say to her Majesty that she wished 'to remain in that estate I was [in], which of all others best like enthused me … As showing her highness I so well like this estate, as I persuade unto myself there is not any kind of life comparable unto it.' Pope then enquired as to whether or not she would marry if an honourable match were put forward. 'What I shall do hereafter I know not, but I assure you upon my truth and fidelity, and as God be merciful unto me, I am not at this present [time] otherwise minded than I have declared unto you, no, though I were offered to the greatest prince of all Europe.'

A year later, it was evident the Queen was dangerously ill, probably from cancer of the ovaries. Her last year was filled with unhappiness. Once more Mary had thought herself to be pregnant, she even added a codicil to her will, passing the Crown to the 'heirs, issue and fruit of my body according to the laws of the realm'. But again there was no child. Philip whom she truly loved, had been away from England for much of her reign. Furthermore, the country was still in financial straits, and unhappy with the Queen's reign. Calais – an English possession for more than two hundred years, and vital both strategically and commercially – had been lost. Philip, wishing to maintain his links with England and perceiving that the Queen's life was in danger, instructed Count Feria, one of his most trusted diplomats, to ingratiate himself with Elizabeth.

As soon as it was known that Mary was dying, the roads to Hatfield were choked with traffic: 'many personages of the Kingdom flocked to the House of Miladi Elizabeth, the crowd constantly increasing with great frequency.' Elizabeth retreated to Brocket Hall, the house of her neighbour Sir John Brocket. Count Feria visited her there. 'We laughed and enjoyed ourselves a great deal', he reported to Philip:

I gave her to understand that it was Your Majesty who had procured her recent recognition as the Queen's sister and successor, and not the Queen or the Council, and this was something your

Background The park surrounding Hatfield, in which, according to tradition, Elizabeth was standing or sitting beneath an oak tree when a number of privy councillors came to her with the news that Mary had died and she was now queen.

Majesty had been trying to secure for some time, as she no doubt realized, for it was common knowledge in the whole Kingdom; and I condemned the Queen and the Council severely.

Elizabeth must then have been fairly forthright, which was not to Feria's liking:

She is a very vain and clever woman. She must have been thoroughly schooled in the manner in which her father conducted his affairs, and I am very much afraid that she will not be well disposed in matters of religion, for I see her inclined to govern through men who are believed to be heretics, and I am told that all the women around her definitely are…. She puts great store by the people who put her in her present position, and she will not acknowledge that your Majesty or the nobility of this realm had any part in it, although as she herself says they have all sent her assurances of their loyalty …

In fact, Elizabeth had an abiding affection for King Philip and kept his portrait near her bedside for the rest of her days. 'There is not a heretic or traitor in all the kingdom', continued Feria, 'who has not joyfully raised himself from the grave to come to her side. She is determined to be governed by no one.' The conversation eventually turned from serious matters of state to jewellery. They spoke of the jewels Mary had given to Philip at the time of their wedding. Feria pointed out that the jewels Mary received from her husband were more costly. These included a gold-and-enamel insignia of the Order of the Garter, thickly set with gemstones. Philip later offered them as presents to Elizabeth; Feria remembered that Elizabeth liked to receive presents. Inevitably, the topic of marriage was raised. Would she yet consider the Duke of Savoy? Apparently not. 'Four years ago', complained Feria, 'your Majesty could have disposed of Madam Elizabeth by marrying her off to someone of your own choosing. Now she will marry whomsoever she desires and your Majesty has no power to influence her decision.' He then surmised that Elizabeth intended to restore peace with France, thereafter maintaining good relations with both Spain and France 'without tying herself to either party'.

Queen Mary died on 17 November 1558. Elizabeth was at Hatfield. Tradition has it that she had been walking in the park and was standing or sitting under an oak tree when members of the Privy Council came to her carrying Mary's coronation ring. Elizabeth, understanding what this symbolized, knelt down on the grass and spoke: '*A domino factum est et mirabile in oculis nostris*' ('God has done it and it is marvellous in our eyes').

Elizabeth quickly appointed her Privy Council, with William Cecil as Principal Secretary of State. On 20 November, she addressed the new Council in Hatfield's great hall: 'My meaning is to require of you all nothing more but faithfull hearts, in such service as from time to time shall be in your powers towards the preservation of me and this commonwealth.'

Three days later, accompanied by more than a thousand nobles, gentlemen and ladies on horseback, Elizabeth headed for London. Then on 28 November, dressed in purple velvet – the colour of royalty – Elizabeth rode in triumph through the crowded streets to the Tower. The people were ecstatic, cheering and singing; at certain points along the route children welcomed her with speeches and there was 'such shooting of guns as never was heard afore'. On 5 December, she proceeded from the Tower by barge to Somerset House where she stayed until the 23rd, moving on to Whitehall for Christmas. A contemporary analyst wrote of the event:

If ever any person had either the gift or the style to win the hearts of people, it was this Queen, and if ever she did express the same it was at that present, in coupling mildness with majesty as she did, and in stately stooping to the meanest sort. All her faculties were in motion, and every motion seemed a well-guided action: her eye was set upon one, her ear listened to another, her judgment ran upon a third, to a fourth she addressed her speech; her spirit seemed to be everywhere, and yet so entire in herself as it seemed to be nowhere else. Some she pitied, some she commended, some she thanked, at others she pleasantly and wittily jested, condemning no person, neglecting no office, and distributing her smiles, looks and graces so artificially that thereupon the people again redoubled the testimony of their joys, and afterwards, raising everything to the highest strain, filled the ears of all men with immoderate extolling their Prince.

The actual coronation day was chosen by Dr John Dee: Sunday 15 January 1559. It was the time of times to be in London. The previous Thursday, Elizabeth had moved by water in spectacular style from Whitehall to the Tower of London; according to medieval custom, the monarch spent the eve of his or her coronation there. Elizabeth lodged in the state apartments of the White Tower. An Italian observer compared the spectacle to Ascension Day in Venice. For the ceremonies, customs officials had been instructed to impound all crimson silk entering the ports, and sixteen yards of velvet were found for each of the thirty-nine ladies attending the Queen. For Elizabeth, a mantle was made from twenty-three yards of cloth of gold and silver. Eight per cent of the annual

Above and opposite
Elizabeth's coronation portrait, painted by an unknown artist. The painting shows the delicate, young queen with the traditional trappings of monarchy. She wears a jewel-encrusted crown and cloth-of-gold robes lined with ermine. In her left hand, she holds the orb, and in her right hand, the sceptre.

royal income was allocated to cover the cost of the coronation, with further sums set aside for the ten-hour banquet that followed. On the afternoon before the coronation, Elizabeth made the traditional procession from the Tower through the streets, displaying herself at every turn in all her regalia. As she left the Tower she paused and prayed aloud: 'O Lord Almighty and Everlasting God, I give thee most hearty thanks that thou has been so merciful unto me to spare me to behold this joyful day.' The Londoners put on five pageants, and an oration summing up the theme of those pageants: religion, morality, the Queen's right to the throne as daughter of Henry VIII, the hopes for the Queen's reign, and speeches of welcome. Elizabeth listened to each pageant and each speech with great attention, straining to catch the words above the press of the crowds.

On the day of the coronation, the Queen went first to Westminster Hall. There went before her trumpets, knights and lords, heralds of arms in their rich coats, followed by the nobles in scarlet and all the bishops in scarlet. At the Hall, the Queen's apparel was changed. Then the procession continued towards Westminster Abbey. 'All the streets were new-laid with gravel and blue cloth, and railed in on each side.' Elizabeth in a gown of cloth of gold, sat in a chariot draped in crimson velvet, over which four knights held a canopy. She wore her hair long, hanging loosely about her shoulders in the style of a maiden. During the anointing, the Queen was dressed in white. After this point in the ceremony, she was reclothed in purple-velvet coronation robes. The Bishop of Carlisle, who had been selected for the ceremony, asked the congregation if they wanted Elizabeth as their queen: 'Whereupon they all shouted "Yes"'; and 'with the organs, fyfes, trumpets and drums playing, the bells also ringing, it seemed as if the world would come to an end'. As Elizabeth came out of the Abbey holding the orb and sceptre, she smiled so much at the crowds that she 'exceeded the bounds of gravity and decorum'.

From the Prison to the Palace

This portrait painted
on wood is believed
to be of Elizabeth. 'All
sorts of subjects and
people, both noble
and mean' wished to
possess an image of
the Queen for their
houses. After a papal
bull was issued in 1570
excommunicating
Elizabeth, the display
of her portrait became
a mark of loyalty. It
seems the loyal subject
who commissioned
this painting admired
the Queen's virtue
and piety. Here, she
wears somewhat
restrained clothing
in the style of the
1580s, which contrasts
with the lavish and
bejewelled regalia of
her state portraits.
The painting is at
Sudeley Castle.

Here is my hand
My dear lover England
I am thine both with mind and with heart

(from 'A Song between the Queen's Majesty and England, 1559' by William Birch)

In the first year of her reign, the Queen launched a magnificent ship which she named the *Elizabeth Jonas*. She chose the name to commemorate her earlier escape from her enemies, a deliverance Elizabeth believed to be as remarkable as that of Jonas from the stomach of a whale. Memories of danger and imprisonment would continue to haunt the Queen. More than twenty years after ascending the throne, she wrote a prayer in which she thanked God for giving her 'even in my youth knowledge of thy truth and in times of most danger most gracious deliverance, pulling me from the prison to the palace'. Having got to the palace, the Queen's consuming interest was staying in power. Gone were the days of her 'little power' and her 'small power'. Never again would she allow herself to be controlled by anyone – except her subjects. Elizabeth was convinced that to remain on the throne she needed the love of her people. To earn their love, her first task as queen had been to assemble an excellent administration, her Privy Council. With these men, and in particular William Cecil, she worked tirelessly for the welfare of England. It was said that 'in her private way of living, she always preferred her necessary affairs and the dispatch of what concerned the government, before and above any pleasures, recreations and conversation'. During her reign, the nation's financial recovery was advanced, and commerce increased along with global exploration and expansion, all helped by Elizabeth's parsimony and abhorrence of war. In the matter of religion, she re-established Protestantism, while aiming for a balance between Catholics and Puritans. She adopted the title 'Supreme Governor' of the Church, avoiding the more contentious 'Supreme Head' used by her father and her half-brother. She also replaced the 'Second Prayer Book of Edward VI' with the somewhat modified 'English Prayer Book'. Visitors from the

Continent were often surprised to discover that under
Elizabeth so much of the outward ceremony practised in
the Catholic Church had been maintained in England's
Protestant churches. Two other developments of the era
were the extension of education and town self-
government. With increasing education, prosperity and the
cosy stability of a reign that was to last more than forty-four
years, the arts flourished; for inspiration, there was the
Virgin Queen, a concept that was fundamental to the
success of Elizabeth's reign. She did not rely on
government alone to win her subjects' devotion. She
courted the English people by energetically promoting an
image of herself as the mood of the country required: it was
no coincidence that she emphasized her maiden state,
becoming the Virgin Queen, in a country no longer
allowed to openly worship the Virgin Mary. Later on, the
Virgin Queen image was adjusted to suit and encourage a
revival of chivalry. The variations were sometimes subtle,
sometimes bold: virtuous Queen, chaste goddess, mighty
imperial monarch, all-powerful being at one with the
cosmos; the changes kept the romance alive, and Elizabeth
Jonas in the palace.

On succeeding to the throne, Elizabeth inherited nearly
sixty royal houses, including the principal palaces built
along the River Thames in or near London: Greenwich,
Whitehall, Richmond, Hampton Court and Windsor
Castle. Oatlands in Surrey was another residence of palatial
proportions. Beyond the vicinity of London the numerous
great country houses and lesser residences were scattered
across England and Wales, extending as far north as
Northumberland, but were mainly concentrated in the
southern counties. The royal residences in the south
included Otford in Kent, Havering-atte-Bower in Essex,
Reading Abbey in Berkshire and Woodstock in
Oxfordshire. These were occasionally visited by the
Queen, but more often were left in solitude under keepers

Above A miniature painted by Nicholas Hilliard, one of Elizabeth's favourite artists, shows the queen playing the lute, which she often did in her privy chamber with her closest courtiers. She also liked to play 'when she was solitary to shun melancholy'.

who ensured their maintenance while enjoying the use of the parkland and pasture.

The movements of the Court were generally dictated by a seasonal cycle. The Queen was in the country during the summer months, and with the chill of winter the Court returned to Whitehall Palace in London, arriving in time to celebrate Elizabeth's Accession Day on 17 November. The Queen's re-entry to the city was a ceremony of state to which ambassadors were invited. Elizabeth made the most of the occasion, displaying herself in the best possible crowd-pleasing style while sitting alone in an open gilt carriage under a canopy of red velvet embroidered with gold and pearls, and looking 'like goddesses are wont to be painted'. Before her rode the gentlemen of the Court, her chamberlains, bishops and councillors; a great noble bore the Sword of State, and the Master of the Horse, Sir Robert Dudley, Earl of Leicester, led her palfrey. She was welcomed by the Lord Mayor, who was accompanied by hundreds of burgesses wearing gold chains. In the procession for the opening of Parliament, the Queen rode in a sedan chair supported by two cream-coloured horses with yellow manes and tails, which were harnessed with golden trappings. To their manes and tails were fastened yellow and white plumes.

But Elizabeth did not confine her public appearances to formal state processions; to win the hearts of her people she willingly attended London amusements, such as the Christmas programme of horseplay organized by the 'Lord of Misrule', with music, pasteboard dragons, and citizens capering about on hobby-horses. After the Christmas season, which ended on Twelfth Night, the Court moved to Hampton Court, Greenwich or Richmond for the festivities surrounding Candlemas (February 2) and Shrovetide. On the Thursday before Easter, Elizabeth observed the solemn Order of the Maundy, which in 1572 was held in the great hall at Greenwich Palace. The ceremony commemorated the Last Supper, at which Christ instituted the Eucharist, and after which he washed his disciples' feet, and gave them a new commandment that they love one another. During the ceremony at Greenwich, Elizabeth knelt upon cushions and washed the feet of thirty-nine (the Queen's age at the time) poor women from 'a silver basin filled with warm water and flowers'. After wiping the women's feet, she made the sign of the cross above the toes and kissed them. Having administered to the whole thirty-nine, she gave each person gifts of cloth, shoes, a platter filled with fish and bread, red wine and small white purses containing thirty-nine coins. On 1 May, the Queen and the Court climbed the hill behind Greenwich Palace and walked into the 'sweet meadows and green woods … to rejoice [their] spirits with the beauty of sweet flowers and with the harmony of birds'. As well as the dictates of the season and the round of festivals, the Court moved as the palaces required cleaning, 'sweetening' and repairing. The numbers of a full Court during Elizabeth's reign varied between 800 and 1,200 people.

Wherever she happened to be residing the Queen required a privy chamber, a bedchamber, a presence chamber and a guardroom. The greater part of her day was spent in her privy chamber – the inner sanctum – where she transacted government business, met with councillors and received ambassadors. With work cleared away, she sat and chatted with her ladies and a few of her favourites. They listened to or made music, sang, played cards and board games, and read. Elizabeth also took most of her meals in the privy chamber. The royal dinner was brought in by the Yeomen of the Guard – 'clothed in Scarlet, with a golden Rose upon their Backs' – to the music of two kettle-drums and twelve trumpets, which made the hall 'ring for half an hour'. A countess rubbed gilt plates with bread and salt, then gave the Guard morsels from each dish – joints of beef, all varieties of game, pasties and tarts – as a precaution against poison. In solemn procession, the dishes were then taken by the Queen's ladies to Elizabeth, who picked at her food or ignored it. She was a finicky eater, taking only a few simple meat dishes with beer or wine. The latter was mixed three parts water to one part wine. 'Precise hours of refection she observed not, as never eating but when her appetite required it.' Lack of appetite may have been due to the consumption of sweets, which she liked to nibble on, eventually causing her teeth to turn black. Some ladies blackened their teeth to appear more like the Queen. Knowing her weakness, courtiers gave her presents of gold-and-enamel comfit boxes.

Below A small, delicate vellum-on-card painting shows Elizabeth (*front left*) performing the Maundy Thursday ceremony in around 1565.

From the Prison to the Palace

Beyond the privy chamber in the principal palaces lay a medley of private or 'secret' rooms, variously consisting of a library, a withdrawing chamber, a bathroom, and a privy gallery opening on to the Queen's privy garden – another private space – in which she talked, thought and walked in relative solitude. Elizabeth was an inveterate walker, regardless of weather. In the company of her ladies she walked briskly; in the company of an ambassador or some other dignitary, she glided along with commanding stateliness.

The privy chamber was principally staffed by ladies whose duties involved handling the Queen's clothes, jewels and some furnishings. Close friends and relations of the Queen were given positions directly attendant upon her person.

The ladies of the bedchamber were nearest and, therefore, most important; in 1559, they were Blanche Parry, Kat Ashley, Lady Katherine Knollys and Elizabeth Norwich. Both Kat Ashley and Blanche Parry, in turn, also held the title of 'Chief Gentlewoman'. Elizabeth's maids of honour were high-ranking ladies who gave service by amusing the Queen, attending at meals and holding the Queen's train as she strutted in the privy garden. They usually numbered six, were attractive and dressed in white – at least towards the end of the Queen's reign; black, always a favourite colour of Elizabeth's, was the permitted dress for mourning. Lady Mary Howard blundered by dressing too fine; Elizabeth mocked the girl before the other ladies and confiscated her velvet suit with its rich border of pearls – no one was allowed to outdress the Queen.

Marriage was another sensitive area: Elizabeth preferred her maids to remain spinsters. If one of the ladies wished to

Below One of the chairs used by Elizabeth's maids of honour when they were at Court attending to her needs. The Queen herself is believed to have embroidered the cushion, a detail of which is shown opposite. The chair is in the drawing room at Loseley Hall in Surrey.

From the Prison to the Palace

marr— it was necessary to consult the Queen, who would be displeased, but might in time, and with great diplomacy, be brought to agree. Mary Shelton, who had married without the royal consent, got her ears boxed. Lady Bridget Manners was guilty of the same offence; her husband was sent to prison. Elizabeth was responsible for her maids, and reprimands were sometimes the result of their dallying rather too freely with the handsome young men at Court. She acted as their mother, guarding their chastity, and they were her '*familia*'. 'When she smiled,' wrote her godson John Harington, 'it was pure sunshine that everyone did choose to bask in if they could'; but when she was angry 'the thunder fell in monstrous measure on all alike'. The mood swings also encompassed love. To grieving friends she wrote letters full of tenderness, and she was protective and loyal towards her maid and close friend Blanche Parry, who had been blind for years. When Blanche died, Elizabeth gave her a funeral befitting a minister of state: her epitaph proclaimed that she, like her mistress, had lived and died a virgin. But the Queen loved Anne Russell, Countess of Warwick, more 'than any other lady or woman'. And she was never too important or too busy to make time for her godson John Harington. While he was still a schoolboy at Eton, she sent him a copy of the speech that she made to Parliament in 1576. Her accompanying letter reads:

Boy Jack,

I have made a clerk write fair my poor words for thine use, as it cannot be such striplings have entrance into parliament Assemblies as yet. Ponder them in thy hours of leisure and play with them till they enter thine understanding; so shalt thou hereafter, perchance, find some good fruits thereof, when thy godmother is out of remembrance …

Her speech to Parliament included the enigmatic phrase 'in being, not in seeming, we may wish the best'.

'Gentleman of the Privy Chamber' was a title given to both John Ashley, Kat Ashley's husband, and Sir Christopher Hatton. It was an honorary position requiring attendance upon the Queen during Court functions. The appointment guaranteed direct access to Elizabeth and with it an opportunity to attract the Queen's bounty in the form of monopolies, property and professional advancement. Courtier Christopher Hatton's career soared from Captain of the Guard to Lord Chancellor, one of the most prestigious positions in the country – and for which, as it happened, he had been an excellent choice. His desire to be near Elizabeth was also personal, and in spite of his eventual greatness,

Hatton continued as a gentleman of the privy chamber until his death. There were also grooms of the privy chamber, who dealt with the practicalities of keeping the Queen's private rooms in order, and the gentleman usher, who scrutinized entrants and etiquette. In spite of her occasional temper tantrums, the privy chamber of Elizabeth's era was a haven of calm and stability, unlike previous and subsequent reigns. The fact that the majority of the staff were women – therefore unable to lead factions – distanced the Queen from individual causes and political crises. Beyond the political storms, Elizabeth was better able to manipulate conflict and make well-considered, independent decisions. Although political power at Court meant access to the sovereign, admittance to her presence was granted only to those in favour; those who misbehaved were firmly excluded.

The privy chamber was connected by a gallery to the presence chamber, which was available to anyone entitled to appear at Court: gentlemen, courtiers, suitors, ambassadors, bishops – all waiting for the Queen's coming forth. The Yeomen of the Guard were deployed to line the route as Elizabeth passed from room to room. 'Before the Queen marched her lifeguard, all chosen men, strong and tall … then came the gentlemen of rank and the Council.' Overseeing the presence chamber were the gentlemen pensioners. Welsh nobleman Lord Herbert of Cherbury recalled his début in the chamber in 1600 when he was a boy of seventeen:

As it was the manner of those times for all men to kneel down before the great Queen Elizabeth, I was likewise upon my knees in the Presence Chamber when she passed by to the Chapel at Whitehall. As soon as she saw me she stopped and, swearing her usual oath, demanded 'Who is this?' Everybody there present looked upon me, but no man knew me until Sir James Croft, a Pensioner, finding the Queen stayed, returned back and told who I was …

Many adventurous young gallants spent a fortune on fashionable clothes and made their way to the Court. To be noticed by the Virgin Queen, as Cherbury had been, was the stuff of dreams.

On rare occasions, the Queen dined publicly in the presence chamber with elaborate ceremony at the board of estate. After dinner, which finished in the afternoon about three o'clock, she liked to watch or join the dancing held in the presence chamber or to dance with a few couples in the privy chamber. When she watched, she reclined on piles of cushions, clapping her hands and tapping her feet in time to the music, occasionally getting up to correct those whose

Right Elizabeth and her courtiers enjoy one of their regular dances. Right up until old age, the Queen would join the lively dancing before occupying herself with the more serious affairs of state. The painting hangs at Penshurst Place in Kent.

From the Prison to the Palace

footwork was not quite up to scratch. But dancing was not strictly an afternoon activity; there were mornings when she danced 'five or six galliards' before settling to work, and she was particularly proud of her robust ability to dance 'high', making great leaps and jumps into the air. Elizabeth kept on dancing, even in old age, just as she kept on hunting and hawking, pushing her wiry frame to the limit. When she became ill she was annoyed: she regarded all maladies as a weakness and a personal insult. 'And she would show herself abroad at public spectacles, even against her own liking, to no other end but that the people might the better perceive her ability of body and good disposition, which otherwise in respect of her years they might perhaps have doubted.'

Off the gallery leading to the presence chamber were the council chamber and the royal closet – the Queen's chapel – usually comprising two rooms, housing an altar in one, and a kneeling desk or similar furniture in the other. The overall management of the privy chamber and the presence chamber belonged to the Lord Chamberlain, who was also responsible for Court entertainments and public ceremony. A special department under the control of the Lord Chamberlain was known as the Office of the Revels, which was in charge of Court pageants, plays and masques. Masques combined theatrical spectacle with music and dance, supporting a theme that usually complimented the monarch. They had evolved from medieval pageants and mummings – exaggerated religious performances for moral instruction and entertainment. Elizabeth carried on the tradition of splendour and spectacle, but in accordance with her policy of retrenchment, they were less lavish than the productions of her father's Court, those of Edward VI's Court or those of the Court of James I, her successor; the Queen preferred being the recipient of entertainments rather than the provider. The actors in the plays were appointed from the companies of men and boys playing publicly in London; Elizabeth organized her own company of players in 1583. An officer from the Office of the Revels gave the actors their parts to learn, and over a period of a few weeks they rehearsed, put on the plays during Christmas or some other festival, and were paid. Sometimes, plays and masques were brought to the Court by amateurs such as the gentlemen of the Inns of Court and Sir Robert Dudley, Earl of Leicester. He was the first to have in his service a company of players, the same group of actors that Shakespeare later joined when it became the Lord Chamberlain's company. In the evening, after supper, masques were danced by the lords and ladies, whose costumes, and those of their attendant torch-bearers, were made and supplied by the wardrobe of the Office of the Revels, as was a wondrous assortment of props. The accounts for the Office of the Revels for the Christmas and New Year's celebrations of 1573–4 include payments to the 'Mercer' for 'Crimsen sarcenet [fine silk] branchte all over with silver … bought cheefely to make Clokes for the foresters mask'. The 'Sylkweaver' provided 'bonelace of copper sylver', fringe, twists, tassels, paper for patterns and leaves for trees, white feathers and curled feathers. The draper provided 'canvas for houses for the players & for other properties as Monsters, greate hollow trees & such'. He also supplied blue silk, white tinsel, thread of every colour, gloves, buttons, hatbands, spangels, cord to truss baskets, and endless other items. The grocer was paid for confections distributed in a masque by 'wild men': sugar, almonds, preserved quinces, walnuts, cloves to stick in pears, cinnamon and ginger, pears made of marzipan, apples, lemons and marmalade. It seems that hair was also made for the wild men, who carried or wore 'mosse and yong Okes … and Ivy'.

One of Elizabeth's favourite palaces was Greenwich. She was born there – as was her father – and her grandmother, another Elizabeth, had been involved in its design. The riverside frontage of the palace was distinguished by mullioned bay windows beneath a crenellated roof. A protruding tower contained the privy apartments, their ceilings gilded and floors strewn with rushes. A visitor to the palace admired a few of the many gifts to Elizabeth, among them were:

a pure silver game of chess and a wolf game [of silver gilt], in which a wolf and a number of sheep [were] played, … a silver-gilt escritoire, … a salt-cellar in the shape of a native decked out with fine feathers, on his shoulders was a shell inlaid and set with pearls and precious stones, [and] … three candlesticks held on high by three men standing on three tortoises … [and] two fine large globes of heaven and earth.

There was also 'a cover [tablecloth] of peacock's feathers sewn together into pretty pictures, and on a sideboard, a cover worked in silver showing the Queen in a carriage over which was written '*Non dolo sed virtute clara*' ('Renowned not for guile but for virtue'). The privy apartments gave direct access to the water – the most convenient travel route. Elizabeth had several barges at her disposal. The Queen's particular barge was powered by twenty men-at-oar, with an interior decorated with coats of arms, cushions of cloth of gold, a blanket of crimson velvet, and a carpet of flowers. When the Queen travelled by river, oily perfume was burned to camouflage the odours that constantly reeked from the Thames. Elizabeth's nose was highly sensitive to unpleasant smells: one unfortunate gentleman was greeted with 'Tush man, your boots stink!' From her privy lodgings on the river's edge, Elizabeth liked to wave to her ships and sailors, who saluted with cannon fire as they passed by. Captain Thomas Cavendish sailed his ship the *Desire* up the river, passing Greenwich Palace and displaying before the Queen a show of booty he had taken from the Spanish. 'His mariners and soldiers were clothed in silk, his sails of damask, his top-masts cloth of gold, and [his ship carried] the richest prize that ever was brought at one time into England'.

London, with around 200,000 inhabitants, was one of the largest cities in Europe, the centre of professional life and the site of Elizabeth's most frequented palace, Whitehall. It had originally belonged to the See of York and was occupied by Cardinal Thomas Wolsey until his downfall in 1529, when it was taken over by Henry VIII and massively altered to receive Anne Boleyn as queen in 1533. Linking the precincts of Westminster with Westminster Abbey and Westminster Palace, Whitehall Palace was a jumble of buildings with some two thousand rooms sprawling over twenty-three acres divided by King Street, which ran between Westminster and Charing Cross. The street was straddled by two gateways: one, which according to eighteenth-century antiquarians was designed by Hans Holbein, had crenellated towers and chequered brickwork; the other comprised rounded towers, Ionic pilasters and classical pediments. The gates connected the domestic and administrative buildings of the palace proper to the palace's park, which was laid out with a recreation centre of four tennis courts, two bowling alleys, a cockpit, a pheasant yard and a gallery overlooking a tilt-yard (an arena in which tilts, or jousts, were held). The exteriors of the main buildings of the palace were covered with decorative paintwork: the hall was immediately discernible with its bold imitation chequerwork, and the outside walls of the privy gallery were painted with black-and-white 'antick' grotesques 'in the forms of different Natures, or Sexes, or Sirenes, Centaures and such like'.

Grotesque-work also extended indoors: it appeared on the ceiling of the privy gallery, which was 'marvellously wrought in stone with gold', and on the wainscott [panelling] of carved wood representing a thousand beautiful figures'. In 1598–9, it was recorded that Elizabeth had at Whitehall 'yerdes square of Draperie worke [a technique that looked like imitation drapery]' painted 'uppon brycke and plastered wall', probably in a gold colour. The ceiling of the Queen's bedchamber was entirely gilt, the bed itself 'ingeniously composed of woods of different colours with quilts of silk, velvet, gold and silver embroidery', and 'hung with Indian work of silk painted on one side'. In the same room, there was 'a table covered with silver and a chair entirely fashioned out of cushions'. Beyond the bedchamber was a 'fine bathroom', where 'the water pours from oyster shells and different kinds of rock'. The room adjoining the bathroom housed 'an organ on which two persons can play duets, also a large chest completely covered in pure silk and a clock which plays tunes by striking on bells'. Next to this was the room 'where the Queen keeps her books, some of which she wrote herself'. On the wall of Elizabeth's privy chamber was an enormous painting by Holbein of the Tudor dynasty: Henry's prominent figure left viewers 'abashed, annihilated in his presence'. There was also an instrument made of mother-of-pearl and inscribed with Latin verses reading:

Dance, true-born sons of England, dance you of Ireland's Isle,
Play upon Orpheus' instrument in tunes of varied style:
Carry the praises of our Queen over the rapid airs
Since she, another Mary, has relieved us from our cares.

The 'Queen's Garden' at Whitehall was rectangular in shape, and bounded by brick walls. At the centre of the garden was a fountain with 'a remarkable sundial, showing the time in thirty different ways'. The plot was divided into raised beds contained within low brick walls. Along the low walls, enclosing the beds, were rails painted in the Tudor colours of green and white. The beds contained herbs and spices to fill the air with a delicious bouquet of scents. Throughout the garden, dispersed in an orderly pattern, were 'thirty-four high columns, carved with various fine paintings; also different animals carved in wood, with their horns gilt … set on top of the columns, together with flags bearing the Queen's arms …'. Between the beds were 'fine walks grown in grass, and the spices are planted very artistically, surrounded by plants in the shape of seats'. To the south was the 'Orchard Gallery', decorated with murals depicting Henry VIII's coronation and the 'Field of Cloth of Gold', the meeting place near Calais where in 1520 Henry VIII and Francis I negotiated in a golden tent. Above the 'Orchard Gallery' ran the 'Stone Gallery', and to the west was the privy gallery.

During Elizabeth's first year as queen, she was hostess to a memorable entertainment at Whitehall for the visit of the duc de Montmorency. There was a banquet in the garden 'under the long and wide gallery on the ground floor [the 'Stone Gallery'], which was all hung with gold and silver brocade', and 'closed with wreaths of flowers and leaves of most beautiful design, which

Right and opposite
Scattered throughout the gardens at Whitehall and Hampton Court were several high, painted columns on which stood wooden heraldic beasts holding flags bearing Queen Elizabeth's coat of arms. The element of pageantry in Elizabeth's gardens was coupled with 'taste, vision and smell' with 'gladsome birdsongs and splashing fountains [to] please the ear, indeed it [was] like an earthly paradise'.

Opposite Railings
painted in the Tudor
colours of green and
white, similar to those
shown here, outlined
the gardens of
Whitehall Palace and
Hampton Court. The
gardens contained
fragrant herbs forming
intricate knot
patterns; the spaces
between the knots
were filled with
coloured sands, or
with flowers such
as primroses,
violets, sweet-
williams and gilly-
flowers (carnations).

gave a very sweet odour and were marvellous to behold'. After the banquet, the Court moved to the tilt-yard gallery, 'so that the said terrace was on all sides beset with Lords, Ladies and persons of quality, sumptuously apparelled and richly furnished; and among them, both above and under, stood many of the Guard in their rich coats, holding an infinite number of torches … by which means those that beheld the terrace in this sort furnished, deemed it rather a Theatre Celestial than a Palace and earthly building'. The gentlemen taking part in the tilt entered the yard 'armed at all pieces', one group of twelve combatants were dressed in silver or white against the others 'apparelled all in blue'. At a signal from the Queen, the competition by torchlight commenced: 'it was 'a sight exceeding glorious … as can hardly be seen the like in any Christian Court'.

To the north of Whitehall's recreation buildings lay an area of parkland leading to St James's Palace – the lesser house previously associated with Prince Edward – which Elizabeth rarely occupied for any length of time during her reign. It was used to house part of her wardrobe, her jewels and other furnishings. She occupied the royal lodgings at the Tower of London – generally used for coronations – even less. As well as its function as a place for keeping prisoners, it was also used as a storehouse for arms and armour, furnishings, jewels and plate. One of the Tower's curiosities was its menagerie: a wolf, a tiger, a porcupine, six lions and lionesses; one lion was named 'Edward', and a lioness was called 'Elizabeth'.

Up river, west from London, lay Richmond Palace, a comfortable residence and Elizabeth's particular favourite during winter's coldest months. Viewed from the river, it appeared as a vast cluster of domed towers enclosed behind a brick curtain wall. Upon each of the towers or turrets was 'a vane of the King's Arms painted and gilt with rich gold and azure'. As the wind blew, the vanes played a kind of music 'marvellous to know and understand'. The palace covered ten acres, and comprised gardens, courts, service buildings, a great hall, a chapel and privy lodgings. The privy lodgings and chapel were distinctively constructed of stone (or brick with stone dressings), whereas the lesser buildings were of brick. Elizabeth referred to Richmond as her 'warm box' or 'warm nest', probably because of its covered passages from one building to another, which meant that it was not necessary to go outside and cross the courtyard in order to enter a building on the opposite side. These 'extended goodly passages and galleries' were 'paved, glazed and painted, beset with badges of gold, as roses, portcullisses and such other'. Recent excavations reveal that the upper walls of the royal apartments were ornamented with a frieze composed of terracotta plaques painted blue. This decoration was probably only on the interior walls since blue was the most valuable of pigments during the Tudor period. In 1580–1, Elizabeth had the shutters and embrasures at Richmond painted with colours resembling cloth of gold, and 'yardes [of drapery-work] in gold colour' painted on the walls of the palace's 'Long Gallery'. At the end of

the Queen's reign, a visitor to the palace marvelled at an extraordinary boat-shaped bed with 'curtains of sea water greene'; the quilts and valance were of light-brown tinsel. Elizabeth made another important addition to Richmond Palace: a water closet – the invention of her godson 'Boy Jack', John Harington.

Farther up river, Hampton Court was a regular destination for Queen Elizabeth and the privileged visitors who came to wonder at its famous 'Paradise Chamber', named for its vast profusion of different gems of inestimable value. The room contained a throne surmounted by the 'Canopy of State, made to the order of Henry VIII'. The canopy was embroidered with 'the Royal Arms of England in gold, encircled by the Garter and studded with pearls of stupendously huge size', with a 'diamond hanging from the extreme end of the Garter'. Nearby was a table with a cloth 'embroidered all over with pearls, almost too heavy to lift'. In addition, there were a large number of cushions 'embroidered with pearls and precious stones', and 'a dicing game made of silver and woods', a mother-of-pearl table, a jewelled water clock, a looking-glass decorated with pearls, a chess set made of alabaster, and ivory flutes used by the Queen's musicians. The ceiling was nearly as sumptuous as the furnishings, being decorated with astronomical figures and in one part 'a picture of the Queen being received into Heaven'.

While Elizabeth loathed spending money, she adored receiving presents and surrounding herself with glorious luxury. All at Court were expected to give her New Year's presents, a tradition that had its origins in Roman antiquity. In return, she gave them gilt plate of a value that accorded with their status. Towards the end of her reign, Elizabeth expected to be given presents on her Accession Day and birthday as well. She also received gifts during her summer progresses. If the offerings of subjects were not satisfactory, the Queen did not hesitate to help herself to her host's possessions. On a visit to Lord Puckering, Keeper of the Privy Seal, at Kew, 'she herself took from him a salt [salt-cellar], a spoon, and a fork, of fair agate'.

In another gallery at Hampton Court, there was a great looking-glass made all of gold, and near it an alabaster incense burner. Yet another gallery contained several paintings, including a 'picture of Venus as a lovely young lady' inscribed with 'the characteristics of love'. The Queen's library, as well as 'a good variety of books', housed a number of 'choice regal possessions': a walking-stick made from a unicorn's horn, sticks containing watches, an elk's horn, a horn cup reputed to break if poison were put into it, cases full of gilt

Opposite A view of the River Thames at Richmond painted by an unknown Flemish artist in about 1620. Richmond Palace, with its cluster of domed towers, can be seen across the river.

Left One of the set of tapestries thought to have been purchased by Elizabeth illustrating Virgil's epic poem *The Aeneid*. This tapestry shows the hero of the poem, Aeneas, departing from Carthage at the bidding of the god Mercury. His love, Dido, is overcome with grief.

vessels, a mother-of-pearl casket, a receptacle for combs shaped like a man, and a magnificent keyboard instrument decorated with glass of different colours and studded with jewels. Inside the instrument was inscribed:

Cantabis moneo, quisquis cantare rogaris,

Vivat ut aeternos Elizabetha dies.

(Whoso is asked, I tell you sing: 'May Elizabeth live forever.')

And over the keyboard:

Phoebe ades et modulos cum tractat pollice princeps

Fac resonent placidum tintula corda melos.

(Phoebus be present; and when Her Grace's finger strikes the keys

make the tinkling strings resound with tuneful melodies.)

The eight-hundred-room palace was everywhere hung with tapestries. Henry VIII had acquired Cardinal Wolsey's considerable tapestry collection, to which he added several hundred of his own, so that at his death the inventory of the King's possessions listed two thousand tapestries. Elizabeth is thought to have bought the palace's *Aeneid* set of tapestries depicting Virgil's epic twelve-book poem in which the Trojan origin of the Roman people is glorified. 'Book IV' of the poem tells the tragic tale of Dido, Queen of Carthage, who had refused offers of marriage from kings, only to fall in love with a soldier, Aeneas. But Aeneas must follow his duty, and leave Dido in order to found a nation for his people. Devastated, Queen Dido takes her own life and is cremated on a great funeral pyre. Another feature of Elizabeth's apartments at Hampton Court was a fireplace with the inscription '*Vivat regina Elizabetha, in qua fons omnis prudentiae*' ('Long live Queen Elizabeth, in whom is the source of all wise dealing').

The privy stairs off the privy gallery led to the 'Queen's Garden'. Below the windows of her chambers, Elizabeth planted flowers, all neatly set out in a knot garden, and she added new windows to her chambers, perhaps to make the most of the panorama below. The gardens surrounding the palace, transformed in the year of Elizabeth's birth, were her father's show-piece: a privy garden to the south, a public garden to the east, and pleasure grounds to the north, leading to the entrance-way and tilt-yard. As at Whitehall, the privy garden had border rails painted green and white. The garden was scattered with columns supporting heraldic beasts – dragons, lions, harts, hinds and greyhounds – holding gaily painted banners and gilded vanes that glistened in

65

the sunlight. There were no fewer than twenty sundials. Parallel to the privy garden was the pond garden, which contained three fish ponds, each bordered with heraldic beasts. Towards the river, the triangular 'Mount Garden' boasted a 'Great Round Arbour', three storeys in height, and made almost entirely of glass, with a leaden cupola topped with beasts and a great gilded crown. To the north of the palace, a larger arbour, several storeys high, rose up from the 'King's Orchard'. Interconnecting galleries ran from one garden to another, in which 'various busts of men and women' were displayed. Four years before Elizabeth's death, Thomas Platter, a German visitor, was shown around the privy garden. In his account of the visit, he described knots or squares in which grass, brick-dust and sand had been used to set out designs, which were best viewed from above, from the Queen's chambers. He also mentioned hedges and borders of 'hawthorn, bush firs, ivy, juniper, holly, elm … box and other shrubs very gay and attractive'. He was then shown a rather remarkable assembly of topiary figures:

There were all manner of shapes, men and women, half men and half horse, sirens, serving-maids with baskets, French lilies and delicate crenellations all round made from dry twigs bound together and the aforesaid evergreen quickset shrubs, or entirely of rosemary, all true to life, and so cleverly and amusingly interwoven, mingled and grown together, trimmed and arranged picture-wise that their equal would be difficult to find.

From the Thames, Hampton Court first appeared as a forest of cupolas and turrets, with variously twisted chimneys. Along the roof, above the cupolas, were the inevitable beasts proudly holding aloft their banners. The palace itself was constructed of red-painted brick with diamond patterning picked out in black, and three storeys of lattice windows. Cardinal Wolsey had designed the building around two main courtyards roomy enough to

Above An inscription carved in the wall below the privy chambers' windows at Hampton Court reveals the date of Queen Elizabeth's building work: 1568.

Opposite This leaded bay window was added to the Queen's chambers at Hampton Court, perhaps for a better view of the palace's vast gardens, or so that Elizabeth could enjoy the flowers she had planted outside her apartments. Poets sang of her as 'Flora, Empresse of Flowers'.

contain his household of six hundred. Nevertheless, Henry VIII extended and embellished the palace, adding a third courtyard and new lodgings for himself and the Queen; he remodelled the chapel, built a new great hall (almost exactly the same size as the one that stood at Richmond), new kitchens, galleries, and a multiple garderobe [privy] seating twenty-eight side by side. As he was a great sportsman, Henry also put in tennis courts, bowling alleys, a tilt-yard and a hunting park of more than 1,100 acres. Elizabeth added more stables, further extended the kitchens and had a fountain built in one of the main courtyards. It was made of black-and-white marble, and was surmounted by the figure of Justice.

Farther up the Thames, Windsor Castle, another destination in the round of palaces, though less frequented than the others, was admired for the beauty of its setting. Built on a hilltop for defence, it commanded far-reaching views over ploughed fields, meadows, woodlands and the river. Once used by William the Conqueror, the castle was a delight for Elizabethan romantics who preferred to link its history with the legend of King Arthur. The most significant and expansive construction of the castle commenced in the 1350s and was carried out by Edward III, who gave it the appearance of a fortified town with fosses and ramparts. Stretching over thirteen acres, it consisted of three courtyards. The first contained St George's Chapel, named after the special patron of the Order of the Garter (Windsor was the seat of the Order, founded by Edward III in 1349). The second courtyard contained a round tower standing on a mound 'ringed with double walls and ditches'. The third courtyard was 'encircled by splendid palace buildings ... a worthy dwelling place for the Queen's Majesty'. In the centre of this courtyard was a 'raised basin or fountain-head of marble'. Steps led to Elizabeth's private apartments, and in the room containing her bed there was a unicorn's horn, a bird of paradise 'partially yellow' in colour, and 'a beautifully embroidered cushion done by Queen Elizabeth herself in red and white silk'. When Elizabeth wished to confer with her ministers in private, she had them sit with her in an 'upper gallery' on the 'Queen's couch'.

As with most of her residences, the Queen's building works at Windsor involved repairs sporadically carried out as the royal funds allowed. But she also engaged in some more substantial building there. For instance, she built 'two little lodges with stone porches', a gallery in which she took indoor exercise when the weather was bleak, and a terrace. Another of Elizabeth's Windsor projects was to lay out 'a new garden 1,500 feet in length'. The cost of 'makinge

67

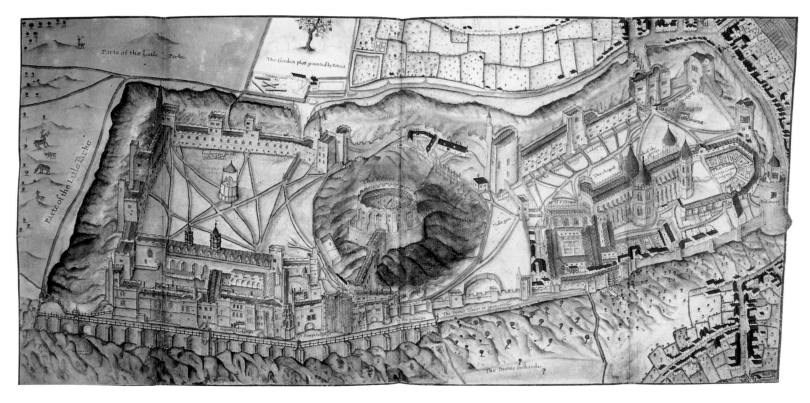

Above A drawing showing Windsor Castle at the time of Elizabeth's reign. The round hilltop tower can be clearly seen in the centre. To the left lies the courtyard in which stood a magnificent 'raised basin or fountain-head of marble'. The gateway to the town appears in the top right-hand corner. The drawing is by Joris Hoefnagel and was produced sometime in the 1560s for Braun and Hogenberg's *Civitates Orbis Terrarum*, an illustrated survey of European cities published between 1572 and 1618.

the gardens perfecte with hearbes growing' was £414.14*s*.8*d*. It also seems that she set aside 'summes of monie to be emploied upon the ornature and alteration of the Mound'. Furthermore, a 'small gateway on Castle Hill, towards the town' bore the inscription '*Elizabethae reginae XIII* 1572'.

One of the Queen's earliest proclamations concerned Windsor Castle, and also one of her chief pleasures – music:

Whereas our Castle of Windsor hath of old been well furnished with singing men and children. We, willing it should not be of less reputation in our days, but rather augmented and increased.

On St George's Day, the Garter ceremonies took place at Windsor, as they still do. Being an entirely masculine event, Elizabeth had the actual ceremonies performed by a deputy, but she willingly attended the plays that were part of the overall occasion. One such play enacted before the Queen at Windsor was 'a most pleasaunt and excellent conceited Comedie' entitled *The Merrie Wives of Windsor*. In 1593, during moments of more solitary recreation at Windsor, Elizabeth amused herself by translating into English *De Consolatione Philosophiae* (Consolation of Philosophy), the work of Roman philosopher Boethius. Though she tackled the project sporadically, it reputedly took the sixty-year-old

Queen only twenty-five days to complete the translation, which was roughly equivalent to 120 printed pages.

With so many residences, it seems astonishing that Elizabeth felt compelled to add to her collection. Yet in 1592 she acquired the Surrey palace of Nonsuch, which like Greenwich became a particular favourite. It had been built by Henry VIII during the last decade of his reign, was sold by Queen Mary to the Earl of Arundel, before passing to John, Lord Lumley, until at last it came back into royal possession. A building of early Tudor Renaissance architecture, Nonsuch was conceived so that there would be literally 'none such' like it – 'aspiring to the very top of ostentation for show'. Elizabeth had earlier appreciated the merits of Somerset House; perhaps it was the aesthetic sensitivity of a connoisseur that prevailed in her need for Nonsuch.

Built upon 'a small elevation' amidst rolling countryside, it was small – more hunting lodge than palace – and intimate; when the Court came to Nonsuch many were necessarily housed in tents. One of its great delights was the 'Inner Court', tucked away like a well-kept secret. The first courtyard was not dissimilar to that of many country houses built by the wealthy of the period, but to pass through the gatehouse leading to the 'Inner Court' was to enter a world of magical surprise. The gatehouse itself boasted two octagonal turrets, and upon its roof stood a clockhouse with 'six gilded horoscopes' and 'a musical concourse of bells' that tolled twice each hour – the prelude to the 'Inner Court'. In the courtyard, visitors were immediately struck by the exterior façade, which was everywhere encrusted, tier upon tier, with white plaster-work depicting the arts, the virtues, gods and goddesses; all along the top were thirty-nine sculptures of Roman emperors. The plaster-work images were fixed into place with richly carved and gilded frames of slate – a glittering composition of white and gold. In the centre of the court, a white-marble fountain with two circular basins was dominated by a white horse poised 'as if leaping up a slope'. Beneath the horse were three maidens, 'the pleasant burden of two golden griffins'. Along the top of the outside walls were decorative battlements sprouting scores of the King's beasts, and there were eighty-five or more chimneys. The 'chief ornament[s]' on the south side of the building were two octagonal towers five storeys high, further extended with domed multiwindowed lanterns; here too the exterior walls were covered with plaster-work figures. Inside Nonsuch, Elizabeth's chambers were decorated with the sumptuousness she favoured in later life: tapestries, hangings of 'red damask embroidered with gold', carpets 'worked in

oru Hoefnagle van Antuuerpen.

Above A painted arabesque panel that may have come from Nonsuch palace. Attributed to Italian artist Toto del Nunziata, who worked in the service of Henry VIII, it represents an early example of the revival of antique grotesque decoration in England. Towards the end of Elizabeth's reign, historian William Camden wrote that there were at Nonsuch 'so many statues and lively images … in every place, so many wonders of absolute workmanship, and works seeming to contend with Roman antiquities'. This panel is now at Loseley Hall in Surrey.

Left A view, painted by Joris Hoefnagel in 1568, showing the approach through the Surrey countryside to Nonsuch, a magical palace acquired by Elizabeth. It was designed and built so that there was 'none such' like it in the whole of the kingdom.

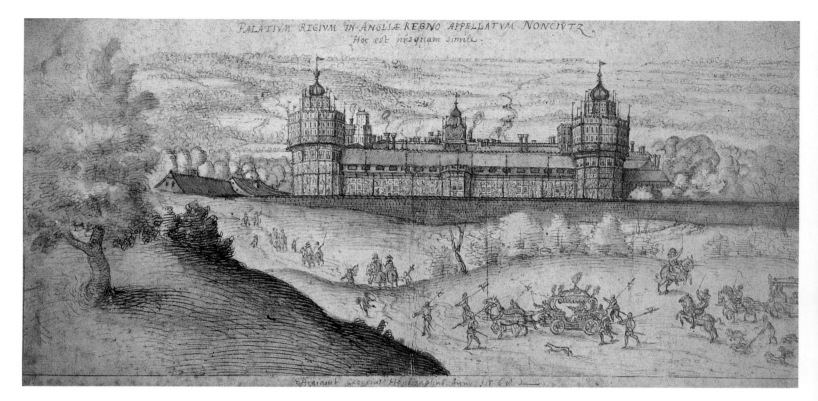

PALATIVM RIGIVM IN ANGLIÆ REGNO APPELLATVM NONCIVTZ
Hoc est nusquam simile.

Effigiabat Georgius Hoefnaglius Anno 1568

Above A pen-and-ink drawing by Joris Hoefnagel shows Elizabeth's stately procession in 1568 through the Surrey countryside towards the southern side of Nonsuch. The two five-storey octagonal towers and the plaster-work covering the walls are clearly visible.

Turkish knot', and piles of cushions. Perhaps less usual was the 'stonework table with 4 containers' effusing red and white wine, beer and water 'when the Queen was present'.

After Nonsuch returned to the Crown, Lumley continued to live there, and laid out an extraordinary garden – 'the finest in the whole of England'. The privy garden was set out in knots around 'many columns and pyramids [obelisks] of marble' with 'two fountains that spout water, one round, the other a pyramid, upon which are perched small birds that stream water out of their bills'. The garden also contained topiary figures similar to those at Hampton Court: 'deer, horses, rabbits and dogs [gave] chase with unhindered feet and effortlessly passed over the green'. One account of the garden mentions a 'large marble wash boule or bason, over which stands a marble pellican fed with a pipe of lead to convey water into the same'. The pelican symbolized the nursing mother who restored life to her brood with her own blood, an emblem often used to glorify the Queen; Elizabeth wore pelican jewels in several of her portraits. In the centre of the garden, built upon a mound was a fountain: 'a shining column which carries a high statue of a snow-white nymph, perhaps Venus, from whose tender breasts flow jets of water into the ivory-coloured marble, and from there the water falls through narrow pipes into a marble basin'. In fact, other accounts and a drawing in the Lumley inventory reveal that the nymph of the fountain was crowned with a crescent moon and therefore represented Diana, the goddess of the moon and the hunt so often associated with Elizabeth, who was herself lyricized by Ben Jonson as 'Queen and huntress, chaste and fair'. Diana was the deity who most definitely presided over the garden at Nonsuch, particularly in the less formal garden, where Lumley created his 'Grove of Diana'. In the centre of the 'grotto or cavern', the story of Actaeon, who was changed into a stag by the chaste goddess, was portrayed 'with great art and lifelike execution'; surrounding the scene was an assemblage of rocks from which water splashed into a basin. At the entrance to the grove were Latin inscriptions charging man to subdue his baser passions. Another feature of the garden was created for the ease of Elizabeth the huntress: a 'platform' constructed from growing shrubs to make an arbour from which, 'either seated or standing, the Queen shoots at deer'. Sir Roy Strong, in his book *The Renaissance Garden in England*, has pointed out that, with such elements as the use of the pelican and the theme of Diana, the garden of Nonsuch formed for the first time in England an 'emblematic tableau which was a standard feature of the Italian mannerist garden'. Just as Somerset House was the first domestic building in England in which classical order was meaningfully transferred from Italy, here too was another first. Elizabeth, who never left England, was nonetheless aware of artistic advances taking place on the Continent, and undoubtedly appreciative of Lumley's efforts at Nonsuch.

Earlier, in the summer of 1559, the previous owner, the forty-eight-year-old Earl of Arundel, had had hopes of marrying Elizabeth, and had attempted to further his suit while entertaining her at his home. He lavished gifts on her, including cupboards of plate, and gave jewels to her ladies. There were banquets served on gilt dishes, and a masque followed by music on flutes and drums, which played into the early hours of the morning. But Elizabeth was immune to Arundel's advances, and never demurred at visiting Nonsuch, either as a guest or later as its owner. In 1599, a visitor to Nonsuch described seeing the Queen:

She was most lavishly attired in a gown of pure white satin, gold-embroidered, with a whole bird of paradise for panache, set forward on her head, studded with costly jewels; she wore a string of huge pearls about her neck and elegant gloves, over which were drawn costly rings. In short she was most gorgeously apparelled, and although she was already seventy-four [in fact

Background A drawing from John Speed's *The Theatre of the Empire of Great Britain* of around 1610 shows the exterior of the buildings surrounding the 'Inner Court' at Nonsuch. The gatehouse to the courtyard, with its octagonal turrets and clockhouse, can be seen in the background. Plaster-work figures decorated all the buildings from top to bottom. The privy garden overlooked by the royal apartments is laid out in neat patterns interspersed with ornaments added by Lord Lumley. The fountain of Diana glorifying Elizabeth can be seen in the centre foreground between the two columns.

From the Prison to the Palace

Opposite The *Pelican Portrait* painted in around 1574 by Nicholas Hilliard. This is one of the several portraits of Elizabeth in which she wears a pelican jewel. The bird, which according to legend pricks its own breast to feed its young with the blood, was used to symbolize the loving relationship between the Queen and her subjects.

sixty-six], she was very youthful still in appearance, seeming no more than twenty years of age. She had a dignified and regal bearing.

Elizabeth's gorgeous apparel was in keeping with her paramount need to attract the admiration of her subjects, which generally meant dazzling them with her majestic attire. Her disdain for spending money did not apply to her appearance; her wardrobe was boundless, and she readily received gifts of clothing from the ladies and gentlemen of the Court: Lady Shandowes gave her 'a dublet of peche collered satten all over covered with white cut worke, and leyed with a lace of Venice gold, lyned with orenged colored sarcesnet [fine silk]'; Lady Sheffield gave 'a dublet of sad tawny satten covered with white cut worke embrawdered with flowers of silver and spangills and lined with white sarcesnet'; the Earl of Warwick gave 'a smocke wrought with black silk, a peire of slevis, and a paratelett [partlet – part of a bodice that covers the chest] wrought with gold, silver, and black silke; her godson John Harington gave 'a peire of sleves and a partelett [partlet] embrodered with gold and silver set with pearles'. Upon retiring, Elizabeth may have slipped into the nightgown made of 'tawny satten, all over, enbraderid, faced with satten like heare collour [tawny-brown]' given to her by Secretary of State, and master of the secret service, Sir Francis Walsingham (a nightgown in the sixteenth century was the attire for relaxation, but not actually worn to bed). The list of New Year's gifts for 1578 included eighty presents of clothing for the Queen; it was at about this period that her taste for extravagance in dress began to soar. Even in 1601, when struggling with a bout of ill health, 'the Queen though very feeble and tottering on account of her illness, nevertheless appeared on this occasion adorned and bedecked right royally'. When an overzealous divine preached before Elizabeth admonishing excess, she stalked away before the man had completed his sermon. Her fondness for silk stockings – she wore a new pair every week – similarly aroused criticism from Puritans, who fretted over the tight, clinging material which revealed a shapely leg and ankle when the skirt was raised. Elizabeth amassed shoes, too, and there were also continuous additions to the royal wardrobe of gloves, fans, muffs, ruffs, handkerchiefs, hats, sleeves, petticoats, round gowns, French gowns, kirtles, safeguards, foreparts, mantles and veils; at the time of her death, she owned upward of two thousand items of clothing. No other monarch in English history has been so fabulously attired, and yet she managed to carry it off stylishly and with aplomb.

The Queen led fashion, and ladies across the land, from the middle classes to the nobility, mimicked her style. The edicts making it illegal to dress above one's station – enforced during Henry's reign – were largely ignored during Elizabeth's sovereignty, though no one dared, and few could afford, to outdress Her Majesty. At Court, elegance was evident in the dress of both sexes. The sombre colours, large trunk and padded codpieces worn by gentlemen in Henry's reign disappeared. Elizabeth's male courtiers were finely dressed in bright colours, jewels and earrings, and were eventually codpieceless. The doublet clung to the torso and, from the 1580s, was padded in front to form a protruding 'peascod' belly extending below the waist. A small ruff encircling the neck in the 1570s became a turn-down collar in the 1580s, and then reappeared platter-sized in the 1590s. In the 1580s, the theatrical Earl of Leicester sported a slashed leather doublet revealing rich, colourful fabric beneath the slits. Towards the end of the reign, the look adopted by Elizabeth's gentlemen companions was more lyrical and youthful, the doublet luxuriously embroidered and set off with jewelled buttons. Trunk-hose became diminutive, covering just a few inches from waist to upper-thigh to emphasize the legs in close-fitting tights; shoes were slender and pointed. The ensemble was completed with a fur-edged coat tossed jauntily over one shoulder.

The metamorphoses in Elizabeth's style of dress, and that of the ladies, was even more dramatic. At first, as Elizabeth gauged the mood of her people, there was little change: cone-shaped skirts, embroidered sleeves, puffs at the shoulder, a simple ruff at the neck. During the latter half of the reign, the look became overtly feminine, with a *décolletage* drawing attention to the breasts, and with vast farthingales in

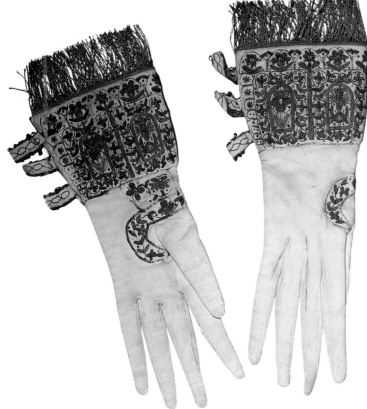

the shape of cartwheels and semicircles worn beneath the skirt exaggerating the hips. The broad skirts were balanced by padded leg-of-mutton sleeves, and huge lace ruffs standing high around the back of the neck, creating a picture frame for the face. Fabrics were densely embroidered, sometimes with images – fish, flowers, birds, foliage – taken from tapestry patterns and sewn with jewels. The look was finished with accessories such as fans, which came into fashion during Elizabeth's reign; she possessed twenty-seven, generally round and made of feathers with costly jewel-encrusted handles. Gloves were another expensive essential, and a popular gift. They had gauntlets, and were embellished with embroidery on the cuffs, tasselled and perfumed. 'Queen Elizabeth's perfume' was made from marjoram, one of her favourite herbs, the leaves of which could be boiled in water to alleviate 'such as are given to over-much sighing'.

Elizabeth was generally regarded as a beauty, in spite of her aquiline nose. Compliments on her looks were always well received, but when they were not forthcoming she herself raised the subject of her attractiveness, and let the flattery flow like honey. As she aged, tactful observers stressed her majesty; the less generous documented her defects, though it is a notable fact that many eyewitness accounts of Elizabeth's appearance in old age remark on her youthfulness. She increasingly resorted to cosmetics as the years passed, resembling a painted doll with false red or yellow hair concealing thinning tresses. Other ladies dyed or sun-bleached their hair in shades of gold to red in order to resemble their queen. An alabaster skin was achieved with a concoction of egg-white, powdered eggshell, alum, borax and poppy seeds, all mixed with mill-water, and also by wearing masks against the sun when outdoors. Belladonna was used to enlarge the pupils.

Having been made-up, coiffured and dressed, Elizabeth was then loaded with jewels: they were pinned onto her ruff and sleeves; looped around her neck and across her bodice; attached to her hair; and hung from her ears. Courtiers contended in the opulence of their gifts of jewellery for the Queen. The lists of New Year's gifts are filled, score upon score, with gem-studded trinkets: the Earl of Ormonde gave Elizabeth 'a feyer juell of golde, wherein ar thre large emeralds set in roses white and red, one bigger than thother two; all threst garneshed with roses and flowers enamules, furneshed with very small diamonds and rubys'; Sir Henry Sidney gave 'a feyer juell of golde with a Dyana, fully

Opposite A pair of the Queen's suede leather boots. Elizabeth had hundreds of pairs of different types of footwear. These boots, known as 'buskins' were worn for riding. Some of Elizabeth's boots were lined with velvet and satin.

Above A pair of Elizabeth's gloves. During her reign, gloves of supple doeskin were an expensive yet fashionable accessory worn by both ladies and gentlemen. During one of Elizabeth's summer progresses the Vice-Chancellor of Cambridge University presented her with 'a paire of gloves, perfumed and garnished with embroiderie and goldsmith's wourke', which must have delighted the Queen for she smiled then immediately put them on.

From the Prison to the Palace

Background A sprig
of marjoram, one of
Elizabeth's favourite
herbs, from which
was made 'Queen
Elizabeth's perfume'.

garnished wythe diamonds, &c'; Sir Thomas Heneage gave 'a proper ringe of golde ennamulled in the top thereof, an white rubye without a foyle, with a grahounde in it'; Sir Henry Lee gave 'a juell of golde, beinge a faire emeraude, cut lozanged hartwise'; and Blanche Parry gave 'a peir of brasletts of Cornelion hedds two perles betwixt every hed, gar with golde'. Another courtier went for practical luxury, giving Elizabeth 'a touthe picke of golde, the top beinge garneshed with a faire emeraude, a dyamond, and ruby, and other smale dyamonds and rubies, with 2 perles pendaunt'. 'O those jewels! The pride and glory of the kingdom', said Sir John Elliot, a Parliamentarian leader, in 1626, in dismay at the actions of King Charles I, who had disposed of Elizabeth's legacy of jewels and plate to raise money. 'Would they were here, within the compass of these walls, to be viewed and seen by us, to be examined in this place [Parliament]! Their very name and memory have transported me.' Sir Francis Bacon refused to be enchanted by the sparkling jewels of the aging Queen, however: 'She imagined', he wrote, 'that the people, who are much influenced by externals, would be diverted by the glitter of her jewels from noticing the decay of her personal attractions.'

Even so, most subjects went along with the fantasy, and continued to adore their virtuous Elizabeth, who glistened almost to the point of incandescence, and aptly fitted the epithet 'Gloriana', as she came to be called in Edmund Spenser's *The Fairie Queene*. The wearing of the Queen's image became fashionable, and was, among English monarchs, unique to Elizabeth. An outward statement of love and loyalty, cameos etched with the image of Augustus had been worn by citizens of Rome as a demonstration of allegiance to their exalted emperor. Similarly, cameos etched with Elizabeth's profile in a costly setting were proudly worn, suspended from a ribbon or chain, or as rings. The reign of Elizabeth was often likened to the golden age of peace and prosperity, the *Pax Romana* of Augustus. The 'Armada Jewel' is a pendant or locket with the Queen's profile on the lid bordered in red, white and blue enamel set with rubies and diamonds. The 'Drake Pendant', which Elizabeth had made for Sir Francis Drake, is set with jewels and a cameo on the outside and opens to disclose a miniature of Elizabeth within; in return, Sir Francis gave Elizabeth a pendant in the form of a ship. Those of limited means showed their loyalty by wearing metal medallions stamped with the Queen's image.

The majesty of Elizabeth's attire is well represented in her portraits, though she tended to dress up for sittings – she was always promoting her image. As she

Opposite The
'Armada Jewel',
which Elizabeth gave
to Sir Thomas
Heneage for his part
in the defeat of the
Spanish Armada. It
opens to reveal a
miniature of the
Queen. The back is
decorated with the
Ark of the true
Church sailing
through stormy seas.

grew older, her portraits were generally less representative of her features, being depicted from established patterns. During the first decade of the reign, there were few portraits of Elizabeth. A painting of 1569, *Queen Elizabeth I and the Three Goddesses*, variously attributed to Hans Eworth, Lucas de Heere or Joris Hoefnagel, shows the Queen in a dress which is richly jewelled, but not unlike those worn by other women of the upper-nobility. At this stage, she relied on allegory, without the support of fabulous clothes and jewels, to carry her message. In the painting, she wears her crown and holds the orb and sceptre while facing the goddesses Pallas, who is 'keen of brain'; Juno, the 'queen of might'; and Venus, 'in beauty shining bright'. On the hill behind the figures is Windsor Castle. The Queen plays the role of Paris, who according to classical legend had to judge which of the three goddesses was the most beautiful, awarding his choice with a golden apple. In this instance, however, Elizabeth leaves the deities confounded, implying that, both as ruler and woman, she herself embodies the qualities of all three: intelligence, power and beauty. It is the earliest known allegorical painting involving the Queen. A few years later, wearing rich, but not extraordinary, Court dress, Elizabeth was portrayed in *The Family of Henry VIII: An Allegory of the Tudor Succession*, a work attributed to Lucas de Heere. In the centre of the painting is the enthroned figure of King Henry, with Edward VI kneeling beside him. To the left stand Mary and Philip II, with Mars, the god of war. On the opposite side and to the foreground stands Elizabeth, accompanied by Peace, whom she grasps by the hand and who tramples on the sword of discord, followed by Plenty bearing an overflowing cornucopia. An inscription on the picture indicates that it was a gift from Elizabeth to Sir Francis Walsingham, an ardent Protestant. After a papal bull was issued in 1570 excommunicating the Queen, the display of Elizabeth's portrait became a mark of loyalty, which probably contributed to an increasing demand for portraiture in general, as well as an increase in the number of official portraits. The style was set by Elizabeth's own conception

From the Prison to the Palace

Right *The Family of Henry VIII: An Allegory of the Tudor Succession*, attributed to Lucas de Heere. This painting, dating from the early 1570s, is one of the earliest to reveal Elizabeth's growing taste for the rich apparel so familiar from her later portraits. The painting hangs at Sudeley Castle.

Below and opposite The *Clopton Portrait*, painted in the early 1560s by an unknown English artist. The sombre mood of this painting is typical of the few portraits made of Elizabeth during the first decade of her reign. Although her dress is undeniably regal, it is restrained, almost Puritanical in comparison with the Queen's later fabulous clothes and jewels.

of majesty: the result of her individual taste and an intuitive understanding of the needs of her people and those of her government.

The characteristic painter of the era was Nicholas Hilliard, Elizabeth's miniaturist, for whom she first sat in about 1572. During one session, she asked him why Italians, regarded as the best painters, avoided shadow in their work. Hilliard replied that shadow was used only by painters whose pictures had a 'grosser line', which was unbecoming to the art of limning. 'Heer', he said, 'her Majestie conseued the reason, and therfor chosse her place to sit in for that porposse in the open ally of a goodly garden, where no tree was neere nor anye shadowe at all ...'. Again Elizabeth displayed an appreciation of continental trends. But then, with regard to portraiture, her aesthetic sensibility seemed to lose momentum, overpowered by the necessity to present a becoming image that was at all times dignified and regal. This was also true of the large-scale portraits. Sweet Sister Temperance, with her serious face, lacking confidence and seeming to watch the artist, vanished and was replaced by a confident, corporate interpretation of majesty, with added allegory and symbolism. In the life-size *Ermine Portrait*, painted in 1585 and attributed to Hilliard, Elizabeth wears a gem-embroidered gown, and strings of pearls, diamonds and rubies. From one necklace is suspended the famous jewel known as 'The Three Brothers', a gem composed of three oblong diamonds set in a triangle around a pointed diamond; each segment is intersected by a pearl, and one great

Left The *Armada Portrait* by George Gower. Three versions of the portrait were painted to celebrate England's decisive defeat of the Spanish in 1588, scenes of which can be seen in the background. The eternally youthful Queen, now dressed in the most sumptuous of dresses and covered from head to toe with jewels, stretches her fingers across the globe: following England's victory over the old enemy, Elizabeth is the empress of the seas. The portrait is at Woburn Abbey in Bedfordshire.

tear-shaped pearl dangles below. She also wears an intricate lacy ruff, a veil of transparent gauze, and a richly bejewelled diadem upon her golden yellow hair. Visible on her left arm is an ermine, another symbol of purity and virginity; the animal wears a gold collar shaped like a crown. On a table next to the Queen is the Sword of State, symbolizing Justice, and in her hand a sprig of olive, symbolizing Peace. England's famous defeat of Spain in 1588 was commemorated in the *Armada Portrait*, of which there are three versions. In George Gower's painting, Elizabeth's gown and two sets of sleeves are embedded with pearls, and several strands of pearls are roped over her bodice. An intricate ruff frames her face, and upon her golden hair she wears a pearl and bejewelled diadem; a single large pearl nestles in her hair just above the forehead. Next to her right arm is an imperial crown, and in the background there are scenes from the defeat of the Armada; her right hand rests upon the globe, her fingers touching the Americas: Elizabeth the Queen is mistress of both earth and sea. The previous year, the first colonial English child had been born on Roanoke Island in the Queen's territory of Virginia, which stretched from what is now the state of North Carolina to present-day Florida. Elizabeth, the imperial votaress, now had nowhere to go but the territory occupied by all-seeing, all-knowing spirits.

The image projected in the *Rainbow Portrait,* painted in around 1600, is one of the most astounding representations of the Queen ever produced; the artist may have been Isaac Oliver. Elizabeth is clad in a gown embroidered with English wild flowers, symbolizing the Queen as Astraea, the just virgin of the Golden Age from classical literature. She is wrapped in a cloak with an orange lining decorated with eyes and ears, indicating fame, or knowledge conveyed to the Queen by her councillors. The poet John Davies wrote: 'Many things she sees and hears through them, but the Judgment and Election are her own.' She is heavily adorned with pearls and rubies, and an elaborate head-dress supports the royal crown; the pearls and crown symbolize Virginity and Royalty, respectively. Above the crown is a crescent-shaped jewel, meaning that in this instance she is Cynthia, another goddess of the moon, whom a poet (probably John Lyly) described as the 'wide ocean's empress' in verses composed for Elizabeth's entertainment. Framing her face is a lacy ruff to which a jewelled gauntlet is attached, perhaps a memento from a significant joust honouring the Queen. Behind her head and around her shoulders is a transparent veil edged with more pearls. Coiling along Elizabeth's left arm is a serpent, which suspends

Above and opposite The *Rainbow Portrait*, painted in around 1600, possibly by Isaac Oliver, a pupil of Nicholas Hilliard. The painting is now at Hatfield House.

from its mouth a ruby in the shape of a heart; above its head is a celestial sphere. The serpent was the traditional symbol of wisdom; here it rules the passions of the Queen's heart. The sphere also implies prudence or wisdom, and together with the serpent and the heart, complements the theme of Astraea. In her right hand, she holds a rainbow with the motto '*Non sine sole iris*' (No rainbow without the sun); the rainbow symbolizes peace. Elizabeth was in her late sixties when this portrait was made, and yet she appears as a curvaceous young woman with orange-gold hair worn in ringlets around her pretty face; goddesses have an advantage over mortals: their beauty is ageless. Portraits that showed Elizabeth as old were ordered to be destroyed. John Davies, in his 'Hymnes to Astraea', written in 1599 to celebrate the anniversary of the Queen's accession, indicated the difficulties placed upon the royal portrait painter in not simply capturing the Queen's image, but also in depicting the correct level of glory:

E xtreme was his audacitie,
L ittle his skill that finisht thee:
I am asham'd am sorry,
S o dull her counterfeit should bee,
A nd she so full of glory.

B ut here are colours red and white,
E ach line, and each proportion right;
T hese lines, this red and whitenesse,
H ave wanting yet her life and light,
A maiestie, and brightnesse.

R ude counterfeit, I then did erre,
E ven now when I would needs inferre,
G reat boldnesse in thy maker;
I did mistake, he was not bold,
N or durst his eyes her eyes behold;
A nd this made him mistake her.

Perhaps the most influential images of the Queen were those on frontispieces to the Bible and John Foxe's *Acts and Monuments*, both of which were widely available. As with the official paintings, these portraits projected a flattering image, which, with accompanying allegorical symbols, told a tale that deified Elizabeth while celebrating her monarchy.

Devotion to the Queen was the very essence of the Court, in which love games – or as one observer put it 'the ordinary infection of this place' – were endlessly in play. And Elizabeth needed to be admired and flirted with: in courtly love she was an enthusiastic participant. During the first half of her reign, there was a certain lustiness in the flirtation; later on, love of Elizabeth became the chivalrous, idealized love of poets for the unattainable. She had her particular favourites: Sir William Pickering; Robert Dudley, Earl of Leicester; Sir Christopher Hatton; William Herbert, Earl of Pembroke; Edward de Vere, Earl of Oxford; Robert Devereux, 2nd Earl of Essex; and Sir Walter Ralegh, among many others. One of the others, Sir Thomas Heneage sent her a bodkin and pendant with the message, '*Amat iste sine fine*' ('This man loves you without end'). She replied with the message, 'I love *sine fine*', giving him 'ten thousand millions of thanks' and promising to wear his pendant near that ear 'that should not hearken to anything that should anyways hurt him that sent it'. And knowing that he was 'far in the cold north country where no butterflies were', she sent him a mother-of-pearl butterfly to ponder. When Sir Thomas died in 1595, he left a jewel to Elizabeth in his will, with the message that it was for her 'who above all other earthly Creatures I have thought most wourthie of all my hartes love and reverence'.

Elizabeth's male companions were generally handsome, the first essential in attracting the Queen's notice, but to maintain her interest – and benefaction – it was also necessary to shine intellectually; the inner circle belonged to 'her deep wits'. The Earl of Leicester was a great patron of the arts and letters, and could engage Elizabeth in endless intellectual discussions; then in the next moment she would burst with laughter over some private joke. She undoubtedly loved him, and coddled him, even fussing over his eating habits. When Leicester visited the Earl and Countess of Shrewsbury, Elizabeth wrote to his hosts advising them to 'allow him by the day for his meat two ounces of flesh … and for his drink the twentieth part of a pint of wine to comfort his stomach, and as much of St Anne's sacred water as he listeth to drink'. On festival days, she advised a 'shoulder of wren, as is meet for a man of his quality … and for his supper a leg

HONI SOIT QVI MALY PENSE

POSVI TOREM
DEVS MEVM
ADIV

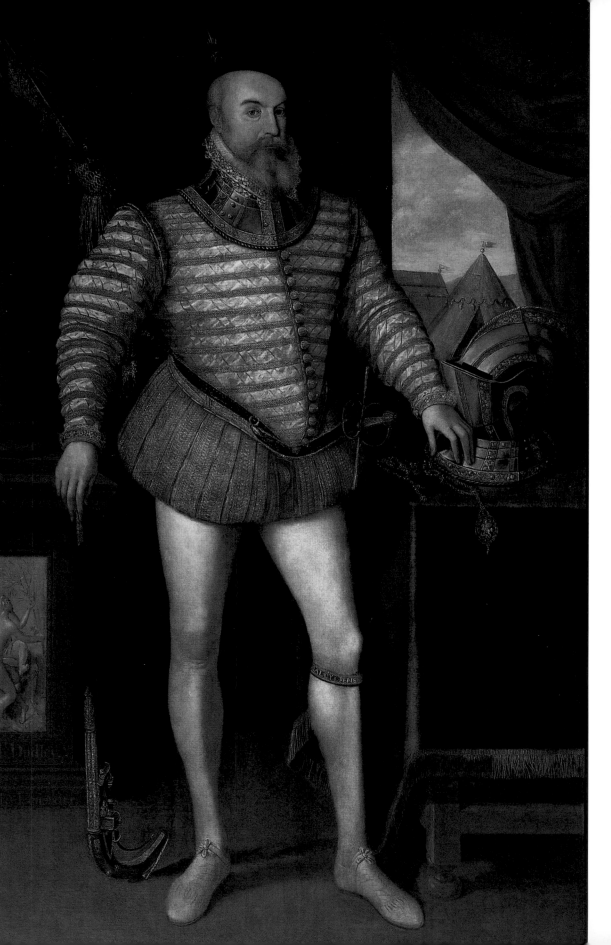

Left A portrait of Sir
Robert Dudley, Earl
of Leicester, the
closest of all of
Elizabeth's male
companions. The
couple's intimacy
was the cause of
much gossip at Court.
They were probably
deeply in love. Today
the painting hangs at
Parham, West Sussex.

of the same'. For many years, marriage between the two was the talk of the Court, as was the inevitable scandalous speculation on the intimacy of their relationship. Sir Christopher Hatton also came in for a share of scandalous talk, the result of his obvious love for Elizabeth. He said of her that: 'The Queen did fish for men's souls, and had so sweet a bait that no one could escape her network.' To historian, explorer, sailor, soldier, courtier and poet Sir Walter Ralegh, the Queen was his beloved moon goddess Cynthia, for whom he felt a certain amount of earthly desire: 'My thoughts are winged with hopes, my lips with love'; and he was not unaware of her attractiveness:

O eyes that pierce our hearts without remorse,
O hairs of right that wears a royal crown,
O hands that conquer more than Caesar's force,
O wit that turns huge kingdoms upside down!
Then Love, be judge, what heart may thee withstand:
Such eyes, such hair, such wit and such a hand.

But the frustration of his passion led to indignation, and he eventually acknowledged the Queen's fading beauty. In response to Marlowe's famous poem 'Come live with me, and be my love,/And we will all the pleasures prove …' Ralegh wrote a sneering parody:

If all the world and love were young,
And truth in every shepherd's tongue,
These pretty pleasures might me move,
To live with thee, and be thy love …

The flowers do fade, and wanton fields
To wayward winter reckoning yields,
A honey tongue – a heart of gall –
Is fancy's spring, but sorrow's fall.

But could youth last and love still breed
Had joys no date, nor age no need,
Then these delights my mind might move
To live with thee, and be thy love.

When Ralegh eventually married one of the Queen's maids of honour, Elizabeth had them both sent to prison.

Below A portrait of poet-adventurer Sir Walter Ralegh and his son painted in around 1600 by an unknown artist. Ralegh made a powerful impression on Elizabeth when he first appeared at Court in 1581. In his *Book of the Ocean to Cynthia*, he describes his complex, tortured relationship with the Queen: 'She gave, she took, she wounded, she appeased'. Yet he played at loving her long after it had become an illusion, for to possess Elizabeth meant 'the world, the power and the glory'.

Thirty-four years the Queen's junior, Robert Devereux, 2nd Earl of Essex, was the man among her close companions who, after the Earl of Leicester, probably meant the most to Elizabeth. She made him feel important and he regarded her as a radiant goddess or fairy, to whom he was tied 'by more ties than ever was subject to a prince', and he bore her 'infinite love'. But he was petulant, and unable to keep his ambition in check. He frequently quarrelled with Elizabeth; she called him a 'rash and temerarious youth', although she always forgave even his most outrageous behaviour. When a question arose regarding the command of an expedition to Ireland, Essex, in a fit of anger, turned his back on the Queen and, according to Ralegh, told her that 'her conditions were as crooked as her carcase'. Elizabeth boxed his ears; Essex drew his sword and stormed out of the Court. In 1601, Essex at last went too far, instigating a senseless, ill-planned rebellion. It cost him his life, and Elizabeth a broken heart. She grieved over the young man's death for the remaining two years of her life, although she had signed the order for his execution.

The love games played at Court, though diverting, and sometimes exhilarating, now and then caused pain: courtiers moaned of their tortured feelings; Elizabeth, too, was among the wounded and lamented her missed opportunities. The following has been attributed by scholars to both Elizabeth and to Edward de Vere, Earl of Oxford. If it was written by the Earl, he intended to imply that it had been spoken by Elizabeth. In any case, the loneliness of an aging queen is evident, and was, no doubt, a reality.

When I was fair and young, then favour graced me,
of many was I sought, their mistress for to be,
But I did scorn them all, and answered them therefore,
Go, go, go, seek some other where, importune me no more.

How many weeping eyes I made to pine in woe,
How many sighing hearts, I have no skill to show,
But I the prouder grew, and still this spake therefore,
Go, go, go, seek some other where, importune me no more.

Then spake fair Venus' son, that brave, victorious boy
Saying: 'You dainty dame, for that you be so coy,
I will so pluck your plumes, as you shall say no more,
Go, go, go, seek some other where, importune me no more.'

Opposite A soldier and a hero, the ill-fated Robert Devereux, 2nd Earl of Essex, was another of the Queen's favourites, despite being thirty-four years her junior. The portrait now hangs at Parham.

As soon as he had said, such change grew in my breast,

That neither night nor day since that I could take any rest,

Then lo, I did repent of that I said before,

Go, go, go, seek some other where, importune me no more.

Marriage was a recurring topic as long as Queen Elizabeth was considered capable of bearing a child: her privy councillors wished to secure the succession – and their futures – and her subjects hoped for continuity. The world's dukes, princes and kings courted the English queen, seeking an alliance with an increasingly prosperous and strategically placed country. Similarly, many of her own noblemen sought the fair royal hand, and the resulting influence which came with it. In her speech to Parliament in 1576, Elizabeth stated that: 'If I were a milkmaid with a pail on my arm – whereby my private person might be little set by – I would not forsake that single state to match with the greatest monarch in the world.' She knew her power rested in her remaining a Virgin Queen. However, her determination seemed to falter between 1578 and 1581, with what amounted to a public declaration of her intention to marry the 'Frog' from across the Channel, Francis, Duke of Anjou, better known as the Duke of Alençon.

In January 1579, Alençon sent his friend and envoy Jean de Semier, Baron de St Marc, to England to woo Elizabeth by proxy. He was a 'choice courtier, a man thoroughly versed in love-fancies, pleasant conceits and Court dalliances'. Elizabeth was delighted with the ambassador, and soon named him her 'monkey'. He entranced her with his charms and the qualities of his master, while making a show of collecting 'love toys' – the Queen's handkerchief, even a nightcap purloined from her bedchamber – to send to the Duke, an 'unmanlike, unprincelike, French kind of wooing'. Elizabeth did not object. At the time of Semier's visit, she was forty-five; Alençon was half her age. She was concerned about the age difference, but not about her physical attraction: 'Seeing the graces which God has bestowed on us', she wrote to one of her councillors, 'we deem ourselves worthy of a prince as great as Monsieur is'. Alençon's appearance on the other hand was reported to be 'void of good favour, besides the blemish of smallpox', but his letters were enticing and Elizabeth invited him to make a secret visit to England to determine whether or not they were in reality suited to each other before making the romance more public. For the Duke's visit, Jean de Semier was

housed in a garden pavilion at Greenwich. Alençon arrived at dawn on
12 August 1579, and, owing to the early hour, Semier suggested that the
young man go to bed. The envoy then wrote a note to Elizabeth saying
that he wished to God she was in bed beside his master. That evening, the
Queen and Alençon spent several hours together; his appearance was
apparently not displeasing for she was visibly delighted in his company. He
was, after all, an experienced lover with a background of notorious liaisons.
Probably more important to Elizabeth, he was also a patron of arts and
literature. The son of Catherine de' Medici, Alençon had grown up in one
of the most decadent courts in Europe, but also one of the most learned and
luxurious, imparting a becoming polish to the young Frenchman and
complementing his ardour.

His visit to Greenwich lasted nearly two weeks, during which he was
entertained at a grand ball, but as the visit was meant to be secret Alençon could
only marvel at the Queen's agile leaps from a hiding place behind a tapestry.
The ruse fooled no one, however, for Elizabeth kept waving girlishly to the
Duke throughout the evening. Her pet name for Alençon was her 'Frog'.
A reported death of a close friend hastened the young man's return to France,
and on the way he wrote three letters to Elizabeth from Dover, one aboard ship,
and three more from Boulogne, all full of love and desperation, and each tied
with pink ribbon. From Boulogne, he sent 'a little flower of gold with a frog
thereon, and therein Monsieur, his physiognomy'.

As the proposed marriage plan to Alençon became more public, the country
became generally outraged. England and Europe still felt the sting of the
St Bartholomew's Day massacre of 1572, in which three thousand Protestants,
including women and children, had been slaughtered in Paris, and ten thousand
more killed in provincial France over a three-week period; it had been
instigated by Alençon's mother and his brother King Charles IX. The Puritan
John Stubbs wrote that the serpent had 'come to seduce the English Eve and
ruin the English paradise'. For his views, he was sentenced to have his right
hand chopped off. Tradition has it that the moment Stubbs's hand came away
he reached up with his left hand and ceremoniously drew off his hat shouting
'God bless Her Majesty', before falling into a faint. The popular courtier and
poet Sir Philip Sidney was equally adamant in opposing the marriage. 'No, no,
most excellent Lady', he wrote, 'do not raze out the impression you have made
in such a multitude of hearts and let not the scum of such vile minds bear any

Below Bowl, Wanli dynasty, dating from between 1575 and 1620, with English silver-gilt mounts from between 1580 and 1600. This bowl was reputedly presented by Elizabeth to her godson Thomas Walsingham. Both the Queen and Sir Francis Walsingham, among others, backed and profited from Sir Francis Drake's voyage of exploration (and plunder) that set off from England in 1577. Among the cargo of a Spanish vessel captured by Drake off the coast of California was a quantity of 'china' to which this bowl has been linked. Today the bowl is at Burghley House in Lincolnshire.

witness against your subjects' devotion'. The controversy continued unabated. Elizabeth wrote to Alençon:

You realize, my dearest, that the greatest difficulties lie in making our people rejoice and approve. The public practice of the Roman religion so sticks in their hearts. I beg you to consider this deeply, as a matter which is so hard for English men to bear that it passes all imagination. For my part, I confess there is no prince in the world to whom I think myself more bound, nor with whom I would rather pass the years of my life, both for your rare virtues and sweet nature … with commendations to my dearest Frog.

This letter crossed with a letter from the Duke in which he delivered the happy news of his mother's blessing and his brother's permission for the match. On to the seal of his letter he stuck a large emerald – a symbol of faithfulness.

During 1580, the courtship was rigorous. Lord Burghley believed Elizabeth intended to marry the Frenchman, so did Hatton, Leicester and many others. Before Alençon's visit to Greenwich, it was said that Leicester had prostrated himself at Elizabeth's feet, begging her not to meet with the Duke. He spread rumours around the Court that Semier was giving her love potions. At one point he even persuaded the Queen's ladies to frighten her with horror stories on the dangers of childbirth to women of advanced age. But despite his efforts, Leicester himself may have been the cause of, or a contributing factor in, Elizabeth's dalliance with Alençon. During the early stages of the relationship with the Duke, the Queen learned from Semier that Leicester had secretly married Lettice Knollys, Countess of Essex – a woman she detested – and that she was pregnant with his child. It was a devastating blow. Elizabeth believed Leicester loved her, or at least that he would have remained loyal by not marrying. The arms and interest of Alençon may have provided needed comfort, and the additional pleasure of arousing Leicester's jealousy. But the all-important mood of the country was such that Elizabeth began to be persuaded that the marriage was impossible, though it seems she struggled before wisdom overpowered her heart. 'See where the love that I bear you carries me', she wrote to Alençon, 'to make me act contrary to my nature quite awry from those who fish in troubled waters to thrust myself in another man's actions'. Though she would not relinquish power to anyone, she had to continue to play the game. The Spanish threat was increasing, and England more than ever needed an alliance with

Right A silver parcel gilt cup thought to have been presented to Sir Francis Drake by Elizabeth in 1582 in recognition of his successful expeditions. The cup is now in the Plymouth City Museum and Art Gallery.

France, though ideally without marriage. 'Here I am between Scylla and Charybdis', Elizabeth fretted to Burghley, 'Alençon has agreed to all the terms I sent him and he is asking me to tell him when I wish him to come and marry me. If I do not marry him, I do not know whether he will remain friendly with me. And if I do, I shall not be able to govern the country with the freedom and security that I have hitherto enjoyed. What shall I do?' This conversation took place in February 1580, when the threat from Spain was being compounded by Francis Drake's plundering of Spanish ships.

In September 1580, Drake returned from the New World with his ships' holds bulging with treasure seized from King Philip's fleet. The investors in Drake's enterprise included Hatton, Leicester and the Queen herself. Before Drake had set off three years earlier, Elizabeth had sent him an embroidered cap and a green silk scarf embroidered with the words 'Thou Lord guide and preserve thee until the end'. Officially, the mission of the voyage had been exploration, but when Drake returned, the profit to investors was calculated at 4,700 per cent (£47 for every £1 invested). The Spanish ambassador was seething, and demanded the return of his country's property, as well as severe punishment for Drake. The Privy Council was at odds over the disposal of the stolen riches. Elizabeth calmed them by suggesting that Drake should come to London to be questioned, and that he should bring with him a few souvenirs from his voyage. On New Year's Day, the Queen proudly wore a crown Drake had given her. It was set with five superb Peruvian emeralds. In April 1581, a magnificent banquet was held aboard Drake's flagship, the *Golden Hind*. The entertainment on board was more sumptuous than any 'since the time of King Henry'. Elizabeth was accompanied by another of Alençon's agents, the Seigneur de Marchaumont. As Drake knelt before her on the quarterdeck, the Queen joked that the King of Spain wanted his head, and raising a golden Sword of State, she motioned as if to strike it off. She then handed the sword to Marchaumont, an unprecedented honour, ordering him to knight Francis Drake, and thus she adroitly drew France into the privateering episode. During Elizabeth's inspection of the *Golden Hind*, her garter slipped down and Marchaumont rushed to claim it for the Duke of Alençon. Elizabeth coyly pointed out that she had nothing else to hold up her stocking, and having retrieved the purple-and-gold garter, she raised her skirt to an immodest level, and replaced it. She later gave the garter to

Marchaumont for his master's collection. Sir Francis Drake gave the Queen a frog ornament made of diamonds.

Also in April 1581, a special banqueting house was erected in the gardens at Whitehall Palace so that Queen Elizabeth, dressed in a gown of gold tissue, could entertain the French commissioners who had arrived to complete the marriage negotiations between herself and Alençon. Traditionally, a banqueting house was generally a small building or structure, located on the roof of a great house or in a garden, in which sweetmeats and fanciful confections were served following dinner. But there was also a regal tradition of more substantial banqueting buildings going back to at least Henry VIII, who had one built at Greenwich Palace. Similarly, Elizabeth's banqueting house at Whitehall was a grand affair, in which banquet foods were served, and various plays and masques performed. It had taken three hundred men, driven hard for twenty days, to construct it in time for the French ambassadors' visit. The building was 'three hundred thirty-two foot in measure', made of canvas and 'painted all the outsides of the same most artificiallie with a worke called rustike, much liked to stone', and lit with 'two hundred ninetie and two lights of glasse'. Inside the banqueting house were several tiers of seats and benches:

and in the top of this house was wrought most cunninglie upon canvas, works of ivie and hollie; with pendants made of wicker rods, and garnished with baie [bay], rue [an evergreen shrub], all manner of strange flowers garnished with spangles of gold, as also beautiful with hanging toseans [interwoven arrangements] made of hollie and ivie, with all manner of strange fruits, as pomegranates, orenges, pompions, cucumbers, grapes, carrets, with such other like, spangled with gold, and most richlie hanged. Betwixt these works of baies and ivie, were great spaces of canvas, which was most cunninglie painted, the clouds with starres, the sunne and sunnebeams with diverse other cotes of sundry sorts belonging to the Queen's maiestie, most richly garnished with gold.

While Elizabeth entertained important guests in her banqueting house, songbirds were placed in the bushes decorating the rafters. In 1583, George Gower painted 'personadges' (perhaps gods and goddesses) about the Arches and Pillars of the Banquett house'; five years later, he added a *trompe-l'oeil* fountain upon the west wall of the banqueting house 'in sundrie oyle coulleurs and … guilded with fine goulde'. Though seemingly an ephemeral piece of architecture, it was one of the most significant buildings Elizabeth commissioned, and certainly the most romantic. But was it a symbol of love, the etiquette of monarchs, or merely part of a political tactic? Whatever the purpose, it was built amid the mounting squalls of controversy emanating from the Court and the country, and surrounding the pedestal of the Virgin Queen. Just after the completion of the banqueting house – mostly funded by Sir Francis Drake's exploits – Elizabeth wrote to the Duke of Alençon: 'I am resolved to end my days with this sole desire, that you think of me always as I plan to be, drawing no other aim but to be pleasing to you.' In her efforts to please, she had several articles of gilt plate, inherited from her father and grandfather, along with gifts from courtiers, melted down so that her goldsmith could create the new, more fashionable, dishes, bowls, trenchers, platters and spoons with which the Frenchmen dined. So that the lords and ladies of the Court might be especially splendid in their attire, Elizabeth issued an order in Council that cloth of gold, velvet and silk be sold at a reduction of twenty-five percent.

The highlight of the festivities was a spectacular tournament. As part of the chivalrous pageantry, a 'Fortresse of Perfect Beautie' was built in the tilt-yard at Whitehall Palace. Therein sat Queen Elizabeth, who was playfully besieged by four of her lords proclaiming themselves to be the 'foster children of Desire', and challenging all comers to combat. They met twenty-two defendants, two of which were in the guise of Adam and Eve, and one was dressed as an unknown knight. 'Wooden guns [cannon] charged with sweet powders and sweet waters very odoriferous and pleasant' were 'shot off … verie doleful musicke was played' and 'six staves' were broken. The allegory of Desire versus Virtue was enacted over three days, during which the fortress was bombarded with 'flowers … fancies … devices … as might seem fit shot for desire'. In the end, Virtue triumphed; the impregnable fortress was 'to be reserved for the eye of the whole world'.

In October, the Duke of Alençon himself arrived at Court and stayed for three months. Queen Elizabeth tried to discourage his return to England; she was by then firmly against the marriage. But to save his honour, and the chance of a now necessary alliance with France, she continued to treat him with affection. Alençon, something of a military adventurer, had become a major figure in international politics, aiding the Protestants when it suited him. Sidney described him as 'having Alexander's image in his head, but perchance ill painted'. Nevertheless, Alençon had kept Spain at bay for nearly ten years; Elizabeth had to tread very carefully. Also, she probably had personal reasons for maintaining some tenderness for her 'Frog'. During a highly public moment in a

Opposite and right
Nineteenth-century autotype copies of the miniature portraits by Nicholas Hilliard of Elizabeth and Alençon from the 'Queen's Book of Devotions'. Elizabeth's portrait appeared at the front of the book and Alençon's at the back. The miniatures enclosed six prayers composed by the Queen, two of which she wrote between her first meeting with Alençon in 1579 and his death in 1584. It seems that the Duke was the only man Elizabeth ever intended to marry. She probably wore her tiny prayer book (two inches by three), and the image of her lost love contained inside, at her waist, attached to a jewelled girdle. After forty copies of the book were made in 1893, the original disappeared; the whereabouts of the other thirty-nine copies is unknown.

gallery at Whitehall, Elizabeth kissed Alençon, and the two exchanged rings –
the equivalent of an official engagement. 'You may write this to the King,' she
told the French ambassador, 'that the Duke of Alençon shall be my husband.' A
few months earlier, she wrote that the young man had shown her 'a rare
constancy and affection'. When Alençon left England in 1582, Elizabeth
accompanied him to Canterbury. She had given him £30,000 to help finance a
military campaign in the Netherlands. At their parting, she broke down in
floods of tears. She wrote a sonnet, 'On Monzeur's Departure':

I greeve, and dare not shewe my discontent;
I love, and yet am forst to seeme to hate;
I do, but dare not say I ever meant;
I seeme starke mute, yet inwardly do prate;
I am and not; I freeze, and yet am burn'd;
Since from myself, my other self I turn'd.

Elizabeth ended the sonnet with:

Or let me live with some more sweete content;
Or dye, and soe forget what love ere meant.

In 1582, the amorous correspondence continued. Elizabeth remarked that she
would give a million pounds to see her Frog swimming in the Thames again. In
1583, Elizabeth asked Dr John Dee his view of 'Monsieur's estate'; both
Alençon's health and position had become precarious. Dr Dee told Elizabeth
that Alençon would commit suicide, but on 10 June 1584 he actually died of
fever. Elizabeth wrote condolences to Catherine de' Medici, saying that she
herself could find no consolation: 'Madame, if you could see the image of my
heart you would see a picture of a body without a soul.'

For her private devotion, Elizabeth compiled a miniature prayer book
containing six prayers: two in English, one in Italian, one in French, one in
Latin and one in Greek. The two English prayers were composed between
Elizabeth's first meeting with Alençon in 1579 and his death in 1584. One of
these was the prayer in which she thanked God for pulling her 'from the prison
to the palace'. In the same prayer, she also thanked God:

for placing me as Sovereign Princess over the people of England. And above all this making me
though a weak woman yet thy instrument to set forth the glorious Gospel of thy dear Son

From the Prison to the Palace

Left and below
A book cover
(front and back)
embroidered in the
eighteenth century,
and based on the
design of a prayer-
book cover Elizabeth
made during her life.

Christ Jesus. Thus in these last and worst days of the world when wars and seditions with grievous persecutions have vexed almost all Kings and Countries round about me, my reign hath been peaceable and my Realm a receptacle to thy afflicted Church. The love of my people hath appeared firm and the divizes of mine enemies frustrate.

The size of the prayer book was two inches by three. It was probably encased in rich binding with a jewelled clasp, which Elizabeth wore about her waist, attached to a jewelled girdle. At the front of the book was a miniature of Elizabeth, and at the back, one of Alençon. Both had been painted by Nicholas Hilliard.

The Shrines

Approaching the house, being led by a large, long, straight, fair way,
I found a great magnificence in the front or front pieces of the house,
and so every part answerable to the other, to allure liking'
(Lord Burghley describing his visit to Sir Christopher Hatton's
Holdenby House in August 1579)

Above William
Cecil, Lord Burghley,
painted by an
unknown artist.
Burghley was
Elizabeth's
dependable political
servant for more than
forty years. Though
the relationship was
not always an easy
one for Burghley, he
remained loyal to his
queen until his death.
The portrait now
hangs at Parham in
West Sussex.

Opposite The
innovative, Roman-
style barrel-vaulted
staircase at Burghley
House, Lord
Burghley's ancestral
home in Lincolnshire.
When it was built,
the staircase set
the pattern for
stately ascent.

The transaction of love between Elizabeth and her courtiers, and between
Elizabeth and her subjects, was evident in the vast country houses that began to
appear on the English landscape during her reign. These houses, the like of
which had never been seen before (except, perhaps, Wolsey's Hampton Court),
were tailored to charm Elizabeth with comforts, and each had an element of
fantasy in honour of the goddess aspect of the Queen's persona. For her part,
Elizabeth held out the hope that she might one day visit these edifices,
displaying the spectacle of her monarchy along the way. Although providing
hospitality for the Queen and the Court was a cripplingly expensive business –
quite terrifying for the financially meek – the host was sustained by the
anticipation that Her Majesty's gratitude would take the form of honours and
lucrative benefits. Furthermore, a visit from the Queen was a boon to the status
of even the most socially elevated householder.

One such house frequently visited by Elizabeth was Theobalds (pronounced
'Tibbalds') in Hertfordshire, the property of William Cecil, Lord Burghley, her
partner in politics for forty years. The Cecils had been connected with the
Tudors since William's grandfather fought at the side of Henry Tudor, later
Henry VII, at Bosworth Field in 1485. His father held several minor positions in
the Court of Henry VIII, while William, with the stealth of a professional
politician, managed to secure appointments in the Courts of both Edward VI
and Mary I. In 1550, Elizabeth appointed Cecil her surveyor when she acquired
Somerset House; he had been Lord Protector Somerset's private secretary
during the building of the house. Furthermore, both Elizabeth and Cecil were
well acquainted with the scholar Roger Ascham, Elizabeth's tutor. Even before

Mary's death, Elizabeth had decided to choose William Cecil as her Principal Secretary of State, and at the first meeting of her Privy Council she had appointed him to that position, declaring:

This judgment I have of you, that you will not be corrupted with any manner of gift and that you will be faithful to the State; and that, without respect of my private will, you will give me that counsel which you think best: and, if you shall know anything necessary to be declared to me of secrecy, you shall show it to myself only, and assure yourself I will not fail to keep taciturnity therein. And therefore herewith I charge you.

During Elizabeth's reign Lord Burghley enjoyed three chief offices of state: Principal Secretary of State, responsible for the routine business of the Council and for the administration of foreign policy; Master of the Court of Wards, a lucrative post, since wardship was meant to be one of the chief sources of revenue to the Crown; and Lord Treasurer, responsible for the royal finances. He also presided over the Court of the Exchequer. In all, he served from 1558 until his death in 1598, longer than any minister in English history. Burghley's relationship with Elizabeth was sometimes stressful, sometimes frustrating (due to her interminable delay in taking decisions), but always loyal – on both sides. She wept over his final illness, visiting him as he lay in bed, and feeding him 'with her own princely hand'. A short time before his death, Elizabeth wrote to Burghley that he was 'to her in all things and shall be Alpha and Omega'. She called him her 'Spirit', and was inconsolable when he died.

The profits William Cecil gained during his appointment as Master of the Court of Wards allowed him in 1564 to purchase the manor of Theobalds. The house, intended for his recently born son Robert, was situated near the main road from London to Ware in Hertfordshire, in the vicinity of several royal houses, and *en route* to Burghley House, the Cecil family seat in Lincolnshire. At Burghley House, William Cecil displayed his architectural flair in the construction of the inner courtyard – the entrance façade has a triumphal arch inspired by Somerset House – and, inside, in the creation of the 'Roman' staircase, with its stone, barrel-vaulted ceiling, then unique in England, which set the pattern for stately ascent. But the overall scheme was probably constricted by the use of earlier foundations. This was not the case at Theobalds, Lord Burghley's greatest architectural adventure. Over a period of twenty years, he altered, extended, and then wholly rebuilt Theobalds, 'encrease by occasion of Her Majesty's often coming'. Elizabeth stayed there at least twelve times, for

Left The exterior and grounds of Burghley House.

Right The great hall, Burghley House, built during Elizabeth's reign. At the far end of the hall is a clock, carved in the nineteenth century, the hours of which are indicated by the Latin form of Elizabeth's name, 'Elizabetha'.

periods of three, four and six weeks. The house eventually consisted of five courtyards progressing 'across a quarter-mile access', with several archways and open loggias painted with classical frescos. Through the archways – which were like a series of frames – could be observed the inner, 'Fountain Court' and its marble figures of Venus and Cupid. At each corner of the court was a tower carrying turrets spiked with gilded vanes. Central to Theobalds' complex of courtyards and buildings was the hall, entered through an elaborate Renaissance porch and surmounted by a bell tower.

The house contained five galleries, lit by 'many large and spacious windows', for entertainment and exercise in all weathers. For those who wished to venture a little further, the roofs were 'laid almost level for walks', giving the best prospect of the gardens and the surrounding countryside. For Elizabeth's particular pleasure, nature was brought indoors in the decoration of the presence chamber with its 'shew of old Oaks and such trees with painted leaves and fruit'. The foliage was so convincing that when the windows of the chamber were opened, birds flew into the room 'perched themselves upon the trees, and began to sing'. Above the trees, the ceiling was laid out as a curious astronomical clock, with the signs of the zodiac, sun and stars working in their courses 'by some concealed ingenious mechanism'. Another room contained a grotto made of 'semi-transparent stone, and roofed over with pieces of coral, crystal and all kinds of metallic ore'. Inside could be seen 'a man and a woman dressed like wild men of the woods, and a number of animals creeping through the bushes'. At the base of the grotto stood a bronze centaur, and the whole structure was supported by columns covered 'with the bark of trees'. Another room, the 'Green Gallery', was painted 'round the walls' with trees, one 'for every county in England, and from their boughs hang the coats of arms of those earls, barons and nobles who lived in that particular county'. The 'specialities' of the counties –

Right A Venus fountain at Bolsover Little Castle in Derbyshire, which was built in 1614 for Sir Charles Cavendish. Theobalds had a Venus fountain which may have resembled this one, for borrowing ideas from Theobalds was a family tradition: Sir Charles's mother, the Countess of Shrewsbury, had earlier borrowed designs from Theobalds for use in her own house Hardwick Hall. Theobalds also had a mount with a maze leading to Venus. Both the fountain and the mount may have been tributes to Elizabeth. In some portraits she is shown holding up a jewel bearing the image of a seaborne Venus-Virgo.

Opposite Panelling at Bolsover Little Castle thought to have been copied from Theobalds after William Cecil's death. Theobalds' lifelike trees in the presence chamber were replaced by oak panels 'coullered of a liver couller and richlie gilded with gold, with Antick pictures over ye same, seeled with a plastered frett ceelinge full of gilded pendance hanging Downe'.

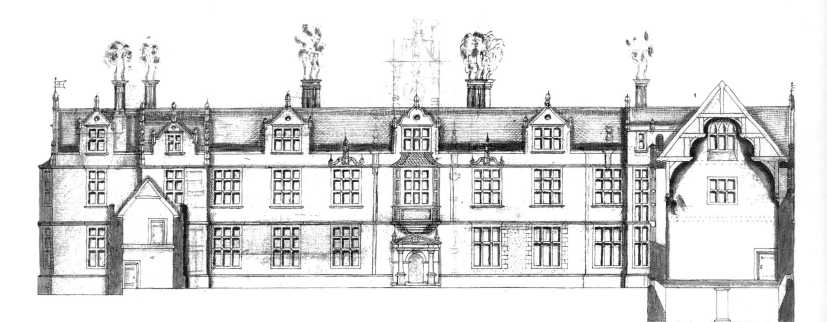

'flocks … herds … fruit' – were also depicted. Lord Burghley was somewhat obsessed with pedigrees – a decorative feature throughout Theobalds – and several coats of arms were set into the house's windows.

Other apartments were entirely 'wainscoted round from ceiling to floor, with architrave, frieze and cornice', and there were 'valuable hangings'; one bed had a 'coverlet woven of gold, another … of ostrich feathers, and hangings made with wonderful skill out of multi-coloured straw'. There was also 'a draughts board with all the pieces made of gold and silver, an oil-lamp made of gold, and a painting on the wall of Queen Elizabeth's coronation'. Lord Burghley was fond of paintings, particularly portraits. At Theobalds, portraits of the Roman emperors, knights of the Golden Fleece, kings of England, dukes and princes of Europe and members of the Cecil family adorned the walls. Burghley's descendants possess a painting entitled *Diana*, which was painted in around 1560 and is attributed to Frans Floris. In the mid-nineteenth century, the work was thought to be a portrait of Elizabeth in the guise of Diana the Huntress, but this is now considered incorrect. Nevertheless, it is the sort of picture Burghley would have displayed at Theobalds as a compliment to the Virgin Queen. Other features of note at Theobalds were its fireplaces, variously made from 'carved freestone cut into Antiques and other wild beasts', alabaster, and black and white marble. The carved wooden staircase was also very fine, embellished with carvings of musical instruments, a motif perhaps inspired by Elizabeth's fondness for music. It still exists today at Herstmonceux Castle in East Sussex, where it was moved after Theobalds was gradually demolished from 1650 onwards.

Right and opposite *Diana*, painted in around 1560, probably by Frans Floris. It was once thought that this was a portrait of Elizabeth in the guise of Diana the Huntress – recognizable by her attributes of crescent moon, bow and arrows, and hunting dog – but this is now disputed. Artists often honoured the Queen by portraying her as a character from classical mythology. The painting is now at Hatfield House.

But all this grandeur in bricks and mortar, stone, marble and glass, and all the imaginative furnishings, were only just equal to the magnificence of Theobalds' gardens. William Cecil had a passion for gardening: 'He greatly delighted in making gardens, fountains and walks, which at Theobalds were perfected most costly, beautifully and pleasantly.' Amongst the Burghley manuscript papers – now kept at Hatfield House – are the garden plans for Theobalds sketched in Cecil's own hand; the herbalist John Gerarde, who supervised the layout of the gardens, dedicated his famous book *Herball* to Lord Burghley in 1597.

The gardens were divided into two main sections: the 'Privy Garden' and the 'Great Garden'. The 'Privy Garden' was moved as the house expanded, and its actual position in relation to the building is difficult to determine; nor are there any contemporary descriptions. However, a Parliamentary Survey of 1650 describes it as being surrounded by 'a pleasant gravel walk planted on its inner edge with a quickset hedge with 26 cherry trees going east, west and north of the said gardens'. Flights of stone steps led down to a grass walk surrounded by another low hedge, and then another, nine feet in height, which encompassed a central square knot. T-shaped buttresses of whitethorn and privet hedge met the stairs, and on all four sides there were entrances to 'a square knot … turned into a complete fashion and shape, with 3 ascents bordered and planted with Tulipps, Lillies, Piannies [peonies] and Divers other sorts of flowers'. At the corners were four 'round arbours with seats in them'.

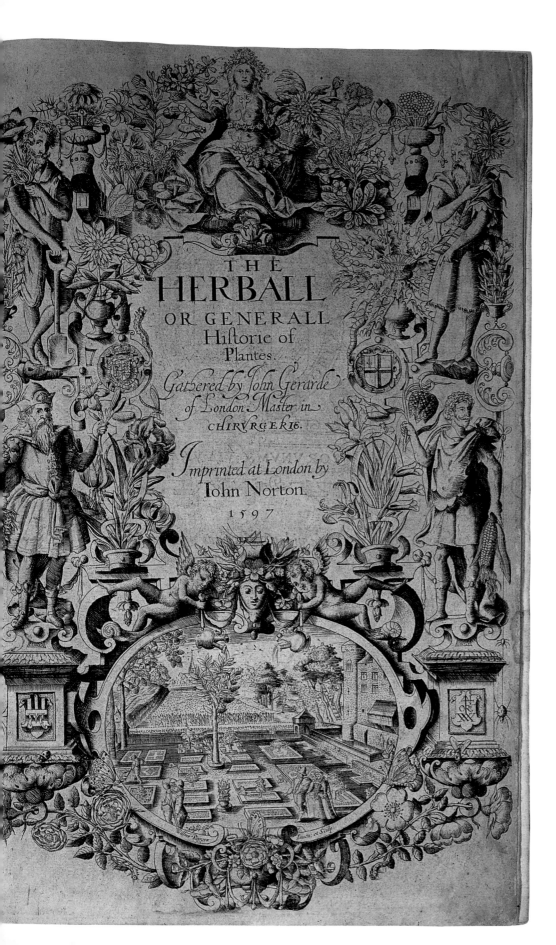

THE
HERBALL
OR GENERALL
Historie of
Plantes.

Gathered by John Gerarde
of London Master in
CHIRVRGERIE.

Imprinted at London by
John Norton.
1597

Left John Gerarde's *Herball*, published in 1597 and dedicated to William Cecil. It is now at Hatfield House

Right and opposite Details of the wooden staircase originally at Theobalds and now at Herstmonceux Castle in East Sussex. The staircase was decorated with carved string and wind instruments and sheets of music, perhaps in honour of Elizabeth's love of music.

Theobalds' 'Great Garden' was aptly named. It covered more than seven acres with arbours, sheltered walks and two miles of manicured pathways. It was surrounded by a wall, and divided into nine knots seventy feet square; walkways twenty-two feet wide ran between the squares. Each knot was 'compassed about with a quickset hedge of whitethorn and privet, and [at] every angle, a fair cherry tree of great growth'. The central knot contained a white-marble fountain. In 1600, a German visitor to Theobalds mentioned that in the centre of the garden was a fountain from which 'water spouts out from a number of concealed pipes and sprays unwary passers-by'. Another knot had an armorial theme; two contained the figures of wild men; and another was 'planted with choice flowers'; the remainder were 'all grass knotts handsomely turfed in the intervalles or little walkes'. The garden was approached through a loggia decorated with genealogies. At various points in the garden were wooden columns; 'alabaster busts of the Caesars'; 'an obelisk of alabaster surmounted by a figure of Christ'; 'an alabaster sundial'; and 'the royal arms of England'. Nearby was a wood with 'a small round hill built of earth with a labyrinth around … called the Venusberg' [a maze leading to the goddess Venus, who, according to legend, presides over an environment of sensual pleasure]'. The mount was probably a tribute to Elizabeth, who, towards the end of her reign, was celebrated as 'Gloriana' – the 'Queen of Love' and the 'Queen of Beauty'. It may have been added by Lord Burghley's son Sir Robert Cecil, Lord Salisbury, who, following his father's death, eventually became Elizabeth's Secretary of State. He inherited Theobalds in 1598, and enlarged the gardens in 1602–3. Another feature of the garden was an ornamental pool into which water flowed 'through the mouths of two serpents'. In two corners of the pool were 'two wooden water-mills built on a rock just as if they were on the shores of a river'. Near the pool, a

summerhouse contained 'marble statues of the 12 Roman emperors … In another room for entertainment, very near this, and joined to it by a little bridge, was an oval table of red marble'. Water was both a visual feature and an entertainment at Theobalds' 'Great Garden'. The pool mentioned above was used for bathing in summer, and the periphery of the garden could be explored from a boat by 'rowing between the shrubs'. This waterway, a sort of moat, was probably joined by a connecting canal to a lake. Unfortunately, these features have now all vanished. But the unfinished garden of Lyveden New Bield in Northamptonshire, begun by its owner, Catholic nobleman Sir Thomas Tresham, in about 1594, with its canals, terraces and mounts – now run wild, though still inviting – conveys an idea of the pleasures to be had at Theobalds. At Lyveden, the mount still rises in a broad gentle ascent, designed for the ease of ladies wearing French farthingales.

It was said of Lord Burghley that: 'His love of his Sovereigne, and joye to enterteyn her and her traine was so greate, as he thought no trouble, care, nor cost too much.' With regard to cost, his expense for the recreation of the Queen and the Court was 'two or three thousand pounds' per visit (about £300,000 to £450,000 in today's money). And such was his attentiveness to her comfort that even the list of foods for her stay in May 1583 received his scrutiny, as shown by the Burghley papers:

Beef	Chickens	Habes	Burra [?]
Mutton	Pidgeon tame	Seafish	Dorye
Veals	Herness [?]	Pikes	Lobsters
Tongues	Shoulders	Carps	Prawns
Bacon	Godwits	Tenches	Sturgeon
Dried Tongues	Pheasants	Breams	Cream
Sheep Tongues	Quails	Eels	Butter*
Pigs	Chics [?]	Roaches	Sweet
Green Geese	Rabbits	Trouts	Eggs†
Capons gr.	Lambs	Oysters	Onions
Capons Good	Venison	Salmon	Scallions
Pullets gr.	Druges	Congar	

★ Some accounts suggest that around 450 pounds of butter were required.

† Some accounts suggest that around 2,500 eggs were required.

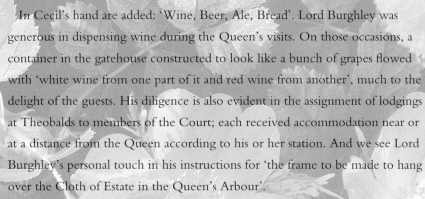

In Cecil's hand are added: 'Wine, Beer, Ale, Bread'. Lord Burghley was generous in dispensing wine during the Queen's visits. On those occasions, a container in the gatehouse constructed to look like a bunch of grapes flowed with 'white wine from one part of it and red wine from another', much to the delight of the guests. His diligence is also evident in the assignment of lodgings at Theobalds to members of the Court; each received accommodation near or at a distance from the Queen according to his or her station. And we see Lord Burghley's personal touch in his instructions for 'the frame to be made to hang over the Cloth of Estate in the Queen's Arbour'.

In May 1591, Elizabeth was welcomed to Theobalds with compliments and speeches. One speech was given by a gardener who described for the Queen a garden that was being designed by Sir Robert Cecil:

It was laid out with flowers symbolizing the twelve Virtues in roses, with the three Graces in pansies, and the nine Muses in nine different flowers … yet all sweet, all sovereign. These mingled in a maze … Then was I commanded to place an arbour all of eglantine, in which my master's conceit outstripped my cunning: "Eglantine", quothe he, "I most honour, and it hath been told me that the deeper it is rooted in the ground, the sweeter it smells in the flower, making it so green that the sun of Spain at the hottest cannot parch it."

There are many allusions in Elizabethan literature to the Queen as 'Eglantine': she is, for instance, referred to as 'Eglantine of Meryfleur', descendant of the kings of Troy. The plant is a variety of sweet-brier, with a single, five-petalled rose in white, or a pink rose that changes to white. In 1590, on the the thirty-second anniversary of her accession, a pillar – symbol of imperial power – was entwined with eglantine and erected in the tilt-yard at Whitehall. Three years later, the poet and dramatist George Peele wrote: 'Wear eglantine/And wreaths of roses red and white put on/In honour of that day'. A symbol of purity, and a favourite emblem of Elizabeth's, the eglantine was used not only in literature, but also in dress, jewellery and paintings. It can be seen, for example, on the 'Phoenix Jewel', which shows the Queen's profile encircled by the plant and tudor roses; Nicholas Hilliard also depicted a young man, thought to be one of Elizabeth's favourites, Robert Devereux, 2nd Earl of Essex, surrounded by branches of eglantine – the inscription on the painting reads: 'My praised faith procures my pain.' In the gardener's speech at Theobalds, the eglantine – and therefore, by extension, the Queen – is greater than the might of Spain.

Opposite Nicholas
Hilliard's famous
*Portrait of a Young Man
Leaning against a Tree*
is thought to show
one of Elizabeth's
favourites, Robert
Devereux, 2nd Earl
of Essex. The figure
is surrounded by
white eglantine.

Below A flower
painting on glass
honouring Elizabeth
as the 'Rosa Electa'. A
Tudor rose is on the
left and eglantine on
the right. Today the
painting hangs at
Loseley Hall.
Elizabeth's gowns
were embroidered
with flowers; they
were tucked into her
hair, and in some
portraits she is shown
holding a flower. She
was also associated
with the flowers of
Spring, meaning
renewal: 'In her shall
last our State's faire
Spring.'

Above The
eglantine's single
five-petalled white
flower was a symbol
of purity and a
favourite emblem of
the Virgin Queen's.

Another of Elizabeth's favourites, Sir Christopher Hatton, built Holdenby House in Northamptonshire 'in direct observation' of Theobalds. He even called upon Lord Burghley to inspect the building while it was under construction. Burghley was duly impressed with what he saw: 'I found no one thing of greater grace than your stately ascent from your hall to your great chamber; and your chambers answerable with largeness and lightsomeness, that truly a Momus [Greek god who found fault with everything] could find no fault. I visited all your rooms, high and low, and only the contention of mine eyes made me forget the infirmity of my legs.' And in comparing Theobalds with Holdenby, Burghley said, 'God send us long to enjoy her, for whom we both meant to exceed our purses in these.' Christopher Hatton was already in debt when he began to build Holdenby, and when he died, fourteen years after Cecil's inspection of the house, he owed £42,000 to the Crown. But no expenditure was too great when it came to building a 'shrine' in honour of his beloved Queen. Holdenby was larger in size than Theobalds and had no equal in grandeur apart from the principal palaces: '… for the bravery of the buildings, for the stateliness of the chambers, for the rich furnishings of the lodgings … and for all other necessaries appertinent to a palace of pleasure, [the house] is thought by those who have judgment to be incomparable and to have no fellow in England that is out of Her Majesty's hands', declared the writer Barnaby Riche after a visit to Holdenby in 1581. But Christopher Hatton had no need for this fabulous house, and he visited it only once in two years; it was all for Elizabeth. He called her 'the Sun that givith light unto my sense and soul'.

Before meeting Queen Elizabeth, Christopher Hatton's lot was similar to that of many young gentlemen of the period. Born in

1540 to William and Alice Hatton of Holdenby, he was left an orphan at the age of six; his education and upbringing may have been the responsibility of a maternal uncle. He entered Oxford University, but left before taking a degree. After Oxford, he pursued the study of law, becoming a member of the Inner Temple in 1560, by which time he had inherited the Holdenby estates. He may have been made a barrister between 1565 and 1567, but he was never either a reader or a bencher of his Inn. It was at one of the Inns of Court that his career of service and devotion to the Queen was initiated with a dance: Hatton's good looks and well-proportioned figure caught the eye of Elizabeth while he danced the galliard for Her Majesty's entertainment. She gave him a place in her personal bodyguard as a gentleman pensioner in 1564. Thereafter he was promoted to Gentleman of the Privy Chamber, and in 1572 he became Captain of the Guard. In 1577, he was made Vice-Chamberlain, given a seat on the Privy Council and knighted at Windsor Castle. From then on, he played an increasingly influential role in government affairs, acting as the Queen's spokesman in the House of Commons. He was also in charge of implementing Elizabeth's religious policy of moderation. In 1587, Sir Christopher was made Lord Chancellor, one of the most prestigious offices in the country.

Though his initial qualifications for government service were questionable, Hatton became a skilful politician and served his country well. The sixteenth-century historian William Camden said Sir Christopher owed his promotions to the 'modest sweetness of his manner'. He was certainly a kind man: amongst his correspondence and other archives are several instances of his generosity and sympathetic nature. The Duke of Norfolk, condemned for high treason as a result of his plan to marry Mary, Queen of Scots, wrote on the eve of his execution to his son: 'Mr Hatton is a marvellous constant friend, one that I have been much beholden unto. Write unto him and seek his goodwill, and I believe you shall find him assured.' The Countess of Derby, who had incurred Elizabeth's displeasure and consequently suffered long imprisonment – without ever actually being accused of any crime – wrote to Sir Christopher beseeching him to intervene with the Queen on her behalf:

Your honourable dealing hath bound me so much unto you as it is unpossible [*sic*] you should make a gentlewoman more beholding unto you than I am....You are the sole person in Court that hath taken compassion on me, and hath given comfort unto my careful heart, and, under

Right A portrait of Sir Christopher Hatton, painted in 1589 by an unknown artist. Hatton's coat of arms appears in the background, including the motto '*Tandem Si*' ('If Ultimately'). The Queen's particular favourites wore about their necks a ribbon, or in this instance a costly jewelled chain, 'with a small gem or intaglio appendant to it; thereon a profile of her majesty's countenance'. Hatton clearly wished to make evident his devotion to Elizabeth.

TANDEM SI

QVI

MAL Y PENSE

HONI SOIT

CASSIS

TVTIS- SIMA VIRTVS

Opposite The dedication page from the *Mariner's Mirror*, published in 1586, and showing Hatton's coat of arms surmounted with a golden hind, the emblem of the Hatton family crest. In recognition of Hatton's generous funding of expeditions, Sir Francis Drake adopted the emblem as the name of his flagship the *Golden Hind*.

God, kept life itself within my brest. All these noble kindnesses are derived from your virtue and good favour towards me, a poor wretched abandoned lady, no way able to yield to you thankfulness worthy thereof.

Musicians, artists and writers also shared Hatton's benevolence. William Byrd, the 'Father of Music', dedicated his *Psalms, Sonnets, and Songs of Sadness and Piety* to him in 1588. In the dedication, Byrd recalled Hatton's fondness for music and hoped that 'these poor songs of mine might happily yield some sweetness, repose and recreation unto your Lordship's mind, after your daily pains and cares taken in high affairs of the Commonwealth'. The artist Cornelius Ketel also received Hatton's patronage, and the era's greatest poet, Edmund Spenser, honoured him in the first sonnet prefacing *The Faerie Queene*:

So you, great lord! that with your counsel sway
The burden of this kingdom mightily

Less well known, the writers Barnaby Riche and Thomas Churchyard dedicated several works to Sir Christopher Hatton. During his role as Vice-Chamberlain, Hatton assisted the Lord Chamberlain in the production of masques and pageants for Her Majesty's entertainment. He also joined the Lord Chamberlain in defending a company of players against the puritanical Corporation of London, whose members argued for the closure of theatres, ostensibly on health grounds, claiming plague was spread in crowded playhouses. In the end, the Privy Council allowed the closure of two theatres: the Theatre and the Curtain. The dismantled materials from the Theatre were used to build another playhouse, the Globe on the south bank of the Thames, of which William Shakespeare was part-owner. In his youth, Hatton acted in masques, and he may have contributed to the writing of at least one masque staged during the Christmas festivities at the Inner Temple. But it was not only the arts that received his patronage: Hatton was also a major investor in voyages of exploration. Francis Drake, in gratitude for Sir Christopher's contributions, changed the name of his flagship from the *Pelican* to the *Golden Hind* – the emblem of the Hatton family crest. Elizabeth's astrologer Dr John Dee, in addition to his other talents, wrote on naval affairs and planned Drake's voyage around the world. In 1576, he dedicated his book *British Monarchy*, or *Hexameron Brytannicum*, to Hatton.

The expenses of Hatton's role at Court, and his patronage of the arts and expeditions, were offset by Her Majesty's generosity in giving him numerous

Opposite A detail of one of the pilasters on the north side of the courtyard at Kirby Hall, one of Sir Christopher Hatton's Northamptonshire houses, which he purchased in 1577 or 1578.

grants of land over the years. In 1568, she leased to him the site of the abbey and the demesne lands of Sulby in Northamptonshire in exchange for his family seat of Holdenby, though on the same date she leased the Holdenby manor and estate lands back to him for a period of forty years. In 1570, she gave him the freehold of Holdenby. He eventually owned or received income from properties in at least eight counties in England. As Keeper of Corfe Castle on the Isle of Purbeck in Dorset, he was endowed with the titles of Lord Lieutenant and Vice Admiral of the Isle. He also enjoyed various monopolies, especially in the wine trade. In Ireland, he had for a few years a monopoly which was 'thought to be of no benefit to that country'.

By 1572, his personal relationship with Elizabeth had become intimate, as is indicated by his letters to her. She called him her 'Lyddes' (the Earl of Leicester was her 'Eyes'), and he often signed his letters to her with the cipher $\wedge\wedge\wedge$. She also called him her 'Mutton', and her 'Bellwither'. He wrote the following in response to her charge of unfaithfulness:

I speak the truth before God, that I have most entirely

loved your person and service; to which, without exception,

I have everlastingly vowed my whole life, liberty and fortune …

In 1573, illness forced Hatton to leave the Court for a period of recovery in Antwerp; Elizabeth had the Court physician accompany him. While he was away, Hatton wrote:

My spirit and soul agree with my body and life, that to serve you is a heaven,

but to lack you is more than hell's torment.…

Would God I were with you but for one hour … passion overcometh me.

I can write no more. Love me; for I love you.

… forget not your Lyddes that are so often bathed with tears for your

sake. A more wise man may seek you, but a more faithful and worthy

can never have you.

… you are the true felicity that in this world I know or find.

In August 1573, he wrote in response to a letter from Elizabeth that it had 'warmed [his] heart's blood with joys above joys'. Even given a broad allowance for courtly language, it would seem that Hatton was very much in love.

While he was convalescing, Elizabeth apparently sent him a jewelled branch, for he wrote that he had received 'the branch of the sweetest bush I will ever wear and bear to my life's end'. The jewels he gave the Queen could have filled a pirate's treasure chest. There was a 'fairy jewel … fully garnished with rubies and diamonds, and flowers set with rubies with one pearl pendant and another in the top'; and 'one flower of gold, containing a great emerald, fully garnished with diamonds, rubies, and three pearls pendant, the one bigger than the rest'. He made such presentations annually. In 1578, he gave Elizabeth a fanciful arrangement of gems described as:

A carcanet [an ornamental collar or necklace] and a border of gold; the same carcanet containing seven red roses of gold, in every of them very small diamonds and in the top a garnet and eight troches of mean pearls, four in every troche, and fourteen pearls pendant, being loose; and the said border containing twenty-four red roses of rubies garnished with a very small diamond in every of them a garnet and pearl pendant …

The Queen's New Year's gift to Hatton was always 400 ounces of silver-gilt plate. The quantity given to even the highest personages never exceeded 200 ounces, and was seldom more than 50 ounces. Furthermore, from December 1576, Elizabeth settled £400 a year upon Hatton for life. The royal bounty that flowed upon him was the cause of much jealousy and suspicion. Inevitably, rumours of the Queen's scandalous behaviour – which had long surrounded Elizabeth and the Earl of Leicester – began to include Sir Christopher Hatton. These rumours infested not only the Court, but were also perpetuated by conspirators against the Queen. In 1571, a man seized for his involvement in a plot to depose Elizabeth quoted a Mr Mather as saying:

The Queen desireth nothing but to feed her own lewd fantasy, and to cut off such of her nobility as were not perfumed and courtlike to please her delicate eye, and place such as were for her turn, meaning dancers, meaning … my Lord of Leicester, and one Mr Hatton, whom he said had more recourse unto her Majesty in her privy chamber than reason would suffer if she were so virtuous and well-inclined as some noiseth her.

However, it seems that in spite of the talk surrounding his relationship with Elizabeth, Sir Christopher Hatton made more friends than enemies.

In keeping with his increased status, Hatton needed a house in London suitably acquitted for entertaining Elizabeth and foreign dignitaries. With Her Majesty's approval, he applied to the Bishop of Ely for the lease of his

house Ely Place at Holborn. The Bishop was unwilling, and dared to disappoint the Queen's favourite, calling forth her rebuke, a morsel of Elizabethan folklore:

Proud Prelate! I understand you are backward in complying with your agreement, but I would have you know, that I who made you what you are can unmake you; and if you do not forthwith fulfil your engagement, by God I will immediately unfrock you.

Elizabeth.

The letter is in fact a forgery printed as a joke in the *London Register* of 1761. However, in tone and intent it matches the letter that Elizabeth had one of her nobles, Lord North, write to the Bishop of Ely. A year later, Hatton received a twenty-one year lease of the Bishop's house. The lease included fourteen acres of land, and the keeping of the garden and orchards. Hatton's rent comprised ten loads of hay, £10 a year and one red rose. Unhappy with only a leasehold on the property, he soon sought, and obtained, the freehold; Ely Place hence became known as Hatton House. Always famous for the beauty of its garden and display of roses, even today the area is known as Hatton Garden, although the medley of modern commercial buildings gives no hint of its former glory. The only remaining building of the period is the small Chapel of St Etheldreda.

In 1577 or 1578, Sir Christopher Hatton purchased Kirby Hall in Northamptonshire, in which he hoped to be honoured with a visit from the Queen during her annual progresses. Now a ruin, the house was begun by nobleman Sir Humphrey Stafford in 1570. A long building with twin bays rising to three storeys, it was constructed around an oblong courtyard containing buttress-like pilasters, then unique in England. The ornamentation on two of the pilasters was copied from a page of architect John Shute's *The First and Chief Groundes of Architecture*, published in 1563, the first English book on architecture. Shute's book, a slim folio containing classical designs freely adapted from the continent, was dedicated to Queen Elizabeth. Hatton altered and extended Kirby, adding more colour and gilt to the hall, putting in a great staircase, and fitting an elaborately decorated barrel-vaulted ceiling to the 'Long Gallery'. The southwest wing, containing the 'Great Withdrawing Chamber', was probably added in anticipation of Elizabeth's stay; sunlight still floods into the room through the large bay windows. The house was modernized by Inigo Jones in the seventeenth century, but had fallen into decay by the beginning of the nineteenth century. Today, Kirby Hall is a romantic ruin inhabited by peacocks,

Right The 'Great Withdrawing Chamber' at Kirby Hall. The southwest wing, in which this room is situated, was probably added in the hope that Elizabeth would visit the house. If she had, she would have occupied this room.

Right A view of the south side of the courtyard at Kirby Hall showing the porch and entrance to the great hall.

Left and far right Giant, buttress-like pilasters on the north side of the courtyard at Kirby Hall, opposite the porch. The pilasters were modelled on designs from John Shute's *The First and Chief Groundes of Architecture*, published in 1563. It was the first book on English architecture, though a text-book adaptation of classical designs from the continent.

Left Kirby's great hall, which Hatton decorated with colours and gilt. Although the house is now little more than a romantic ruin, its previous graceful elegance and 'high sophistication' are still evident.

Background A drawing from John Shute's *The First and Chief Groundes of Architecture*. The folio, which was dedicated to Elizabeth, contained four full-page engravings and one full-page woodcut. Shute had been sent to Italy by the Duke of Northumberland, and upon his return he showed his drawings to Edward VI. But political events and the young King's death meant that the work was ignored until Elizabethan courtiers required new designs to ornament their houses. Employing Shute's designs and those from imported architectural books, they adopted a rather free interpretation of the classical orders, as with the chimneys at Holdenby seen opposite.

Opposite The present-day entrance front of Christopher Hatton's Holdenby House, which he built on his ancestral lands in Northamptonshire. In Hatton's day, this was the kitchen wing.

its elegance nevertheless intact. The architectural historian Sir John Summerson describes Kirby as 'an amazing mixture of bucolic simplicity and high sophistication. Nothing quite like it was seen again.'

But it seems Christopher Hatton was not satisfied with Kirby Hall, for having just purchased the house, he immediately began plans to build another, even more splendid Northamptonshire country house, at his ancestral manor of Holdenby. There, he was not merely embellishing and extending, but creating an entirely new dwelling for a deity. In a letter to Sir Thomas Smith, a member of Elizabeth's Privy Council, Hatton reveals his attitude towards these two houses in relation to Elizabeth: 'I am going to view my house of Kirby, which I never yet surveyed; leaving my other shrine, I mean Holdenby, still unseen, until that wholly Saint may sit in it, to whom it is dedicated.' Instead of replacing or extending the old family manor, Hatton moved uphill and built his palace on a more commanding site. The cartographer John Norden described the location as 'environed with most ample and lardge Fields and goodly pasture, many younge Groves newly planted … Fishe ponds well replenished, a Parke adjoining of Fallowe Deare, with a lardge Warren of Conyes not far from the house'. Indeed, the Holdenby estate was so vast that Hatton was able to turn 300 acres of level land, 200 acres of meadow land and 70 acres of pasture into park.

The house, like Theobalds, had a hall dividing two main courtyards, with prominent turreted towers at each angle, and further towers or pavilions at either end of the central hall. The towers were similar to those surrounding the main court at Theobalds, but were built around two courts instead of one, giving the overall appearance more cohesion. The forecourt to the main block was entered by two archways. The entrance front and main courtyard were richly ornamented with Doric, Ionic and Corinthian columns or pilasters. Along the roof, classical columns in groups of two were used as chimneys, their entablature seeming to support the sky. Surmounting the porch to the hall was a tower with a domed turret; either side of the porch was an open arcade. But it was the south front of Holdenby that was, according to architectural historian Mark Girouard, 'one of the show-pieces of the Elizabethan age' with its '350-feet wall of glass that flashed its thousands of diamond panes on the summit of the hill'. Girouard says that 'Holdenby used glass more daringly than any other house in England, and probably in Europe.' This was 'in direct opposition to the classical tradition and suggested a new and exciting concept. Houses

Opposite The remains of the three tall obelisks that stood in the great hall at Holdenby House. According to contemporary accounts, these stone monuments bore the names and coats of arms of the various noblemen who had their estates in Northamptonshire. A shield design can still be seen on the columns.

Background John Thorpe's ground plan showing the east courtyard of Holdenby House. The great hall, which divides the house's two courtyards, appears on the left of the drawing. At the bottom lies the south front of the house, famous for its massive wall of glass, and containing a gallery on the upper floor.

could become lanterns.' This was all the more daring since glass was in itself regarded as a costly and precious material; it was used in ornaments and jewellery. Another innovation at Holdenby was the double layer of rooms over a large area, not just limited to one courtyard as at Theobalds. This suggested the concept of a great house that was a 'compact mass', 'heavily windowed all round' – as houses became when the courtyard plan began to go out of fashion.

Details of the interior of Hatton's palace are few. Tourist Baron Waldstein, visiting Holdenby in 1600, wrote in his diary: 'Two stone obelisks stand by the 4 steps which lead up to the porch, and the door itself is quite enormously massive.' The royal arms, not Hatton's, appeared over the porch. 'Coming through this porch', said Waldstein, 'you enter the hall; when you go through it the general interior plan of the house is revealed.' Inside the hall the following lines were written above the door, here translated from the Latin:

Fate had deprived me of my old domain
But from its broken ruins, built up new,
Another Fate gave back again
This mansion which you view.
Live Great Elizabeth eternally!
Free giver of such welcome toil to me.

The verse refers to the legal arrangements mentioned above between Hatton and the Queen regarding the ownership of the Holdenby estates. Hatton's 'welcome toil' was the building of his magnificent house. 'In one of the rooms', continued Waldstein, 'displayed on three tall obelisks, are the names and coats of arms of the earls, barons and other noblemen who had their estates in the county.' It seems that these were in the hall, and that they took the place of the traditional medieval screen which separated a house's entrance passage from its hall. Beneath the royal arms was the motto '*Semper Eadem*' ('Ever the Same'); Hatton's own coat of arms had the motto '*Tandem Si*' ('If Ultimately'). The house contained 'beautifully made and extremely valuable chimney-pieces'. One depicted Apollo, the Nine Muses, and Athena and Mercury, all carved out of stone, with four columns on either side; another had Jupiter seated on an eagle and the seven liberal arts. In the same room were the arms of the Earl of Leicester, with the motto '*Droict et Loyal*' ('Right and Loyal').

Holdenby's gardens featured intricate knot gardens laid out on a great platform of earth along the south front. On either side, terraces dropped down the hillside;

one set of terraces led to a rectangular pool, the other to a bowling green. From 'a most craggye and unfitable lande', said John Norden, Hatton had made:

… a most pleasante, sweete, and princely place, with divers walks, many ascendings and descendings, replenished also with manie delightful Trees of Fruite, artificially composed Arbors, and a Destilling House on the west end of the same gardens, over which is a Ponde of Water, broughte by conduit pypes, out of the feyld adjoyninge on the west, quarter of a myle from the same house.

The design of the garden can, at least in part, be ascribed to a Catholic priest named Hugh Hall, known as 'Hatton's

Left A marble statue in the present-day gardens at Holdenby House. The statue guards a leafy, covered walk leading towards an Elizabethan garden recently re-created at Holdenby. Covered walks, or 'close walks' for shade and privacy, were made by training trees or climbing plants over a wooden frame. They were a common feature of Elizabethan gardens.

Opposite The two arches that once flanked the great forecourt to the east front of the original Holdenby House. They are among the few remains of the old mansion still standing.

Priest'. In 1597, Sir Thomas Tresham of Lyveden New Bield wrote to his steward about a gardener in the employ of his sister, and mentioned that he had been trained at Holdenby by a priest who excelled in gardening work. Hatton was rumoured to have Catholic sympathies. However, evidence of his Protestant leanings exists in the nearby fourteenth-century church, which was, and still is, part of the Holdenby estate. There, seven Protestant texts painted on plaster were discovered during repairs to the church in 1862. They are believed to be Elizabethan in date, since the texts are from the 'Bishop's Bible' of 1568. Also of interest is the church's plate, which consists of an Elizabethan cup and cover paten dating from 1570. William Camden recorded that 'in the cause of religion' Hatton was of the opinion that 'neither searing nor cutting was to be used', and accordingly he often interceded to preserve both Puritans and Catholics from persecution.

At the corner of the gardens stood a banqueting house, described by the Parliamentary Survey Commissioners in 1650 as being of 'a goodly fabrick built of hewn stone … consisting of many fair large rooms'. Known as the 'Dairy House', it was designed like a small, self-contained house, built as a single block with square towers – a hint of things to come in English domestic architecture.

Holdenby was later purchased by James I in 1605, but was seized by Cromwell's forces, before reverting to the Crown at the Restoration. In 1650, the trustees for the sale of Crown lands sold Holdenby to a Parliamentarian soldier, Adam Baynes. He demolished Hatton's masterpiece for its materials, making a residence for himself in the kitchen wing. An arch leading to the forecourt of the present house is inscribed with the date 1656, but it looks Elizabethan and may have been redated when Baynes fashioned his house. Apart from this arch, and the remodelled kitchen wing, the only remains of the exterior of the old mansion still standing are two arches that once flanked the great forecourt to the east front; they now appear like two sentries keeping guard over a grassy field.

Today, set up in the church, is a screen that originally came from inside Holdenby House, possibly from the chapel. It is made of carved wood, and is of Doric design, with an arched superstructure carved with lions, scrolls and grotesque heads. Beneath the arch are two Roman soldiers now flanking a cross; it all seems to have once been part of a more elaborate structure. Other woodwork from Holdenby was used to make the church's reredos

Opposite A wooden
lion sits majestically
atop the carved
screen that originally
came from Holdenby
House but is now in
a nearby church.

Below Another
detail of the wooden
screen from
Holdenby House
shows its two, carved
Roman soldiers.
Today, they guard
a cross.

(an ornamental screen covering the wall behind the altar) and a First World War memorial. Another fragment of past glory is the chimney-piece in the library of the present Holdenby House. It is also made of carved wood, with panels flanked by Doric columns. According to an article on Holdenby published in *Country Life* in 1912, 'the panels and pillars of the library chimney-piece are portions of the old work, but strangers to their new position'.

In 1590, Sir Christopher Hatton, by now the Lord Chancellor, 'in an earnest mindfull care for the discharge of his debtes, caused the yere before his death an Inventorie to be taken and a valuation to be made of all his goodes well known nether to be old nor of the meanest stuff', and 'he gave speciall chardge to praise nothing at the uttermost valew but at under rate which was don accordinglie'. Unfortunately, it seems that these inventories of Sir Christopher's possessions no longer exist, and the actual furnishings of Holdenby can only, for the most part, be imagined. That Hatton House in London was 'furnished richely' is the only indication of the Lord Chancellor's taste that can be gleaned from the Hatton family archives.

Sir Christopher Hatton died in 1591 after a long illness. His nephew Sir William Newport (later Hatton) inherited Hatton House, Kirby Hall and Holdenby. In 1591 or 1592, Sir William sold to the Dowager Countess of Shrewsbury three sets of tapestries that had belonged to his uncle. These were the 'Gideon' set of thirteen tapestries; the 'Abraham' set of twelve tapestries; and a set of six tapestries with unknown 'personages'. Some or perhaps all of these probably originally hung at Holdenby; now they can be seen at Hardwick Hall in Derbyshire, the Countess of Shrewsbury's residence. The Hatton shields depicted in the tapestries were concealed with pieces of cloth painted with the Countess's coat of arms, which included Hardwick stags; painted horns were added to the Hatton hinds. Sir William Hatton died in 1597, having scarcely reduced the family debt to the Crown. A marginal note in the Hatton archives states: 'Twenty cart loades of good stuffe [were] carried from Holdenby to Kirbee upon the death of Sir William Hatton.' Thereafter, the finery that had filled the halls and chambers of the Lord Chancellor's houses seems to have been sold, or in some other way dispersed.

Lord Burghley had said that Holdenby was 'consecrated to her Majesty', but she never, in fact, visited her shrine. It nonetheless remained constantly staffed with servants and always had rooms beautifully appointed. Provisions were kept available for the pleasure of whichever important company happened to arrive; Elizabeth was not among them. Before Christopher Hatton's final illness, Elizabeth insisted upon payment of the money he owed. 'It brake his heart', wrote the seventeenth-century preacher and antiquarian Thomas Fuller, 'that the Queen (which seldom gave boons and never forgave due debts) rigorously demanded the payment of some arrears, which Sir Christopher did not hope to have remitted, but did only desire to be forborn. Failing herein in his expectation, it went to his heart, and cast him into a mortal disease.' In an undated letter from Hatton to the Queen, supposedly written on this occasion, he wrote:

If the wounds of the thought were not most dangerous of all without speedy dressing, I should not now trouble your Majesty with the lines of my complaint. And if whatsoever came from you were not either very gracious or grievous to me, what you said would not sink so deeply in my bosom. My profession hath been, is, and ever shall be

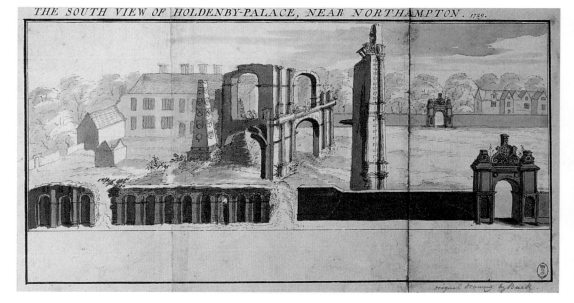

original drawing by Buck.

Right Holdenby House and ruins as seen in 1729. Clearly visible are the two arches of the original Holdenby that still stand today, and one of the three obelisks that were in the great hall. The engraving was done by S and N Buck.

Opposite The elaborately decorated exterior of Wollaton Hall in Nottinghamshire. Rising from the centre of the building is the house's large hall, which is surmounted by a 'great chamber', or 'Prospect Room', with domed turrets at its angles.

to your Majesty, all duty within order, all reverent love without measure, and all truth without blame …

When Elizabeth learned of the seriousness of Hatton's illness, she brought to his London house 'cordial broths unto him with her own hand, but all would not do. Thus no pulleys can draw up a heart once cast down, though a Queen herself set her hand there unto.' When Hatton died at Hatton House in 1591 he was fifty-one years old. Sir Christopher's Holdenby was an exclusive and personal monument to Elizabeth, so much so that he had made only a few brief visits to the house, as if establishing his presence there somehow risked desanctifying the shrine before the Goddess herself claimed Holdenby by crossing its threshold – which she never did. In trying to concentrate emotion within mortar, Holdenby House was England's Taj Mahal.

There were other monuments in honour of Elizabeth. One of the more blatant examples was Wollaton Hall in Nottinghamshire, built not by an elite member of the Court circle, but by a coal magnate and Sheriff of Nottingham, Sir Francis Willoughby, who had hopes of entertaining the Virgin Queen. Wollaton was, and is, a fairy-tale castle, which at first glance appears to have been put together with bits of cardboard, cut paper and pasted-on baubles; it is, in fact, made of stone. Willoughby's vision for this extravaganza may have been conceived during his stay at the Earl of Leicester's Kenilworth Castle in the summer of 1575, on the occasion of the Queen's visit there. For more than two

Opposite A view of the exterior of Wollaton Hall, looking towards one of the corner towers, and showing the stepped appearance of the building.

Right Seen from roof level, a domed turret surmounting the corners of the 'Prospect Room'.

weeks, the Earl's medieval castle glittered with fairy dust, or so it must have seemed during the endless spectacles of Arthurian legend, masques and fireworks staged for Elizabeth's entertainment. While at Kenilworth, Willoughby invited the Queen to visit Middleton, one of his three properties. She apparently declined the invitation, owing perhaps to some inadequacy of the facilities. Whatever the motivating factor, Willoughby decided to build a new, more splendid, house to entice Queen Elizabeth; five years later, Wollaton Hall was begun.

Sir Francis's main criterion for the design was, undoubtedly, to stun onlookers, for the house was unlike anything seen before. It rises to the clouds from the summit of a hill, seemingly in command of all that lies below for miles around. In 1600, William Camden wrote of Wollaton: 'Sir Francis Willoughby knight, out of ostentation to show his riches, built at vast charges a very stately house, both for the splendid appearance and curious workmanship of it.' Wollaton Hall is an 'outward-looking' house – that is, it is without a courtyard – and is nearly square in shape, with square towers at each corner. It was similar to the banqueting house at Holdenby, but on this scale the plan was revolutionary in England. The main north and south walls are offset to accommodate terraces, to which jutting corner chambers have been added, giving the lower tiers of Wollaton a multiwindowed, stepped appearance sweeping upwards to the towers of the outer corners. At the centre of the house, on the ground floor, is a large, enclosed – thus windowless – hall, out of which rises a second square with a clerestory to cast light down upon the hall. This in turn is surmounted by a 'great chamber', or 'Prospect Room', with domed turrets at the angles. The exterior decoration of Wollaton Hall with its strap-work, gables, cartouches, Gothic-type windows, additions to the pilasters and entablatures, is primarily derived from the pages of the works of Flemish architect and designer Jan Vredeman de Vries, though the designs of the Italian Sebastiano Serlio are also evident, as are those of French architect Jacques Androuet du Cerceau. Willoughby owned one of the best collections of architectural books and related works then in existence. The eclectic use of Renaissance ornament certainly adds to the excitement of Wollaton, but it is the 'Prospect Room' that steals the show. Like a mock castle, such as the 'Fortresse of Perfect Beautie' in the Greenwich tilt held in 1581 to impress the French dignitaries then negotiating the marriage between Elizabeth and the Duke of Alençon, the 'Prospect Room' is the main prop in a tale of chivalry. The well-read Willoughby devised his house as the poets of the era devised chivalrous themes complimenting Elizabeth. It is not surprising that Willoughby's brother-in-law the Earl of Arundel was one of Edmund Spenser's patrons: Wollaton Hall appears a fitting habitation for the Faerie Queene. But though Sir Francis Willoughby had such high hopes of entertaining Elizabeth, she never went to Wollaton. If she had, the pomp would have provided great inspiration for a poet.

A house befitting Her Majesty, from a woman's point of view, was, and still is, Hardwick Hall in Derbyshire. It was the triumph of one of the era's greatest builders, the Dowager Countess of Shrewsbury, better known as Bess of Hardwick. Hardwick Hall is similar to Wollaton Hall, with the fairy-tale castle – the chivalrous element – removed. The result is a cohesive stateliness. Bess was born at Hardwick in 1527 to a family of minor gentry. She was married and widowed four times, gaining in social stature and wealth with each marriage. With her second husband, Sir William Cavendish, she had eight children, six surviving infancy. To please her, Sir William bought property in Nottinghamshire and Derbyshire, including the house and estate of Chatsworth, where he pulled down the existing house and built a new one on the site of the present Chatsworth House. The Countess's third husband, Sir William St Loe, held important appointments in Elizabeth's Court, and, as Lady St Loe, Bess had the title of 'Lady of the Bedchamber'. But it seems she had a weakness for idle chatter, and in 1561 she was imprisoned in the Tower for her

Opposite A detail of the screen in the hall at Wollaton. Medieval houses traditionally had a screen or screens separating its entrance passages from its hall. This one is decorated with plaster-work columns, pilasters, figures and intricate strap-work patterns adapted from the designs of Jan Vredeman de Vries.

Below One of Wollaton Hall's impressive corner towers, which rise majestically to the clouds.

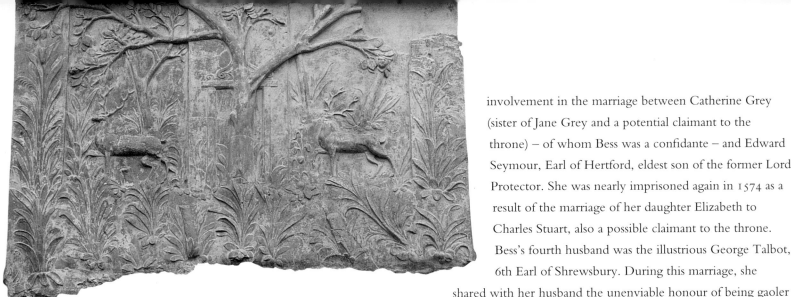

Above A detail of the plaster-work frieze that decorated the 'Forest Great Chamber' of Hardwick Old Hall in Derbyshire, showing deer running through a forest. The plasterer used real branches and leaves to create the forms of the trees on the frieze, which was inspired by a similar decoration at Lord Burghley's Theobalds.

involvement in the marriage between Catherine Grey (sister of Jane Grey and a potential claimant to the throne) – of whom Bess was a confidante – and Edward Seymour, Earl of Hertford, eldest son of the former Lord Protector. She was nearly imprisoned again in 1574 as a result of the marriage of her daughter Elizabeth to Charles Stuart, also a possible claimant to the throne.

Bess's fourth husband was the illustrious George Talbot, 6th Earl of Shrewsbury. During this marriage, she shared with her husband the unenviable honour of being gaoler to Mary, Queen of Scots. Captive and captors were thrown together for fifteen and a half years, which put enormous strain on Bess's marriage, and eventually contributed to its complete breakdown. Indeed, emotions between the Talbots became so bitter that Bess was probably behind rumours accusing the Earl of Shrewsbury of having an affair with the Queen of Scots. In 1584, Mary responded to the gossip by writing a letter packed with venom to Elizabeth. This letter, now among the Burghley papers, was never in fact received by the Queen. Had it been, Bess would have been destroyed, for Mary aimed to wound Elizabeth by attacking her as a woman, and by questioning her fitness to be queen of England. Mary knew how to inflict pain. In the same letter, written in French, the Queen of Scots accused the Countess of Shrewsbury of speaking 'licentiously' against Elizabeth, and of mocking the Queen's need for flattery. She also accused Elizabeth of lying in bed with Leicester; chasing after Hatton; betraying state secrets to Jean de Semier, the envoy of Alençon, whom she allowed the most wanton intimacies, and so on. When the Earl of Shrewsbury was released from his burden as gaoler to retire to his estates, he was reported to have thanked the Queen for delivering him from two devils: the Queen of Scots and his wife. After the collapse of his marriage, Lord Shrewsbury claimed Chatsworth as his rightful property, forcing Bess from the house. Before leaving, however, she stripped the building of its furnishings, to the benefit of Hardwick, where she next concentrated her talents.

Bess had bought the Hardwick house and property from her brother. Today, this house is known as Hardwick Old Hall. In 1587, she began remodelling the house, and added apartments for herself and her son William Cavendish. The interiors were sumptuously decorated with plaster-work, which still in some instances appears remarkably fresh against the now dark and ruined walls of the

Right Plaster-work
figures, thought to
be Geg and Magog,
the legendary forces
of evil, and Eros,
the god of love,
decorating the
chimney-piece
in Hardwick Old
Hall's 'Hill
Great Chamber'.

Old Hall. In the 'Forest Great Chamber', the plaster-work frieze depicts a forest with deer frolicking among the trees. It was the prototype for a similar frieze in the 'High Great Chamber' of Bess's new hall, which she began building in 1590–1, only one hundred yards from the Old Hall. Both friezes were inspired by the original in the 'Great Chamber' of Theobalds. For the Hardwick trees, the plasterer used real branches and leaves for forms. Tall trees were meant to represent constancy. There is a door behind the trees, thought to imply the presence of the faithful subject waiting for Elizabeth to visit, or even of the faithful wife waiting to be invited back to Chatsworth. In the 'Hill Great Chamber' of the Old Hall, the overmantel to the chimney-piece is dominated by giant mailed figures, possibly representing the legendary forces of evil Gog and Magog. They frame a figure of Eros, the god of love, suggesting good conquering evil.

In 1590, the Earl of Shrewsbury died, leaving Bess with a substantially increased income. She was nearly sixty-three years old when Hardwick Hall was begun, and her reasons for throwing herself into another building project are uncertain. She may have anticipated her increased wealth, and the means to make a grandiose statement. Or perhaps she had her granddaughter Arabella Stuart in mind; Arabella, who lived with Bess, had a potential claim to the throne, and a future queen of England would need a magnificent house. Perhaps the improvements to the Old Hall had not met Bess's expectations, since it was a hotchpotch of irregularities and misalignments. In the hope of avoiding past mistakes, she chose an architect of high reputation, Robert Smythson, to put her ideas for the new house into a well-crafted plan. Wollaton Hall had been an earlier Smythson show-piece, though there was also much of Willoughby's individual personality in it. The unity of Hardwick, however, suggests that owner and architect thought as one. Bess expressed

Opposite The exterior of Hardwick Hall, seen from the ruins of nearby Hardwick Old Hall. The large number of draughty windows won the house the rhyme 'Hardwick Hall, more glass than wall'.

Above The carefully manicured gardens of Hardwick Hall as they appear today. Despite the Countess of Shrewsbury's efforts to honour Elizabeth at Hardwick, the Queen never visited the house.

Above A detail of the painted plaster-work frieze representing Diana the Huntress in the 'High Great Chamber' of Hardwick Hall.

herself in the ornamentation, displaying her initials at every opportunity along the roof. Hardwick was ready for occupation in 1597. The most revolutionary feature of Hardwick Old Hall had been the great hall, which was a two-storey chamber, crossing the centre of the house in a position quite different from the traditional medieval design. This treatment was repeated in the new house with great effect. But Hardwick's most outstanding feature – walls of windows – was taken from Holdenby House. Though Holdenby had twice the window surface, Hardwick won the rhyme 'Hardwick Hall, more glass than wall'.

In spite of its endless, draughty windows, Hardwick Hall must have seemed to contemporaries a study in comfort. It was lavishly furnished with Chatsworth treasures and carpets, and filled bottom to top with tapestries and other needlework made by Bess, by her ladies, or by professional embroiderers; even now the house has a feeling of being upholstered. Consideration for comfort

was also given to the main staircase, which winds gracefully in gentle stages, so that one need not arrive breathless at the state rooms on the second floor. The Hardwick coat of arms appears everywhere imaginable: on overmantels, furniture, walls, tapestries and cushions. A stag wearing a collar of eglantines was the Hardwick family crest; three eglantines also formed the upper half of the Hardwick coat of arms. Bess no doubt enjoyed using the emblem favoured by Elizabeth, and she incorporated it in much of her needlework. A table in the 'High Great Chamber' displays the Hardwick stags supporting the motto:

The redolent smele of Aeglantyne
We stagges exault to the devyne

The 'High Great Chamber' itself is the most spectacular room in the house, and a great tribute to Queen Elizabeth. It was designed with the frieze, tapestry and chimney-piece all fitting together. The plaster-work frieze shows Diana the Huntress, surrounded by her Court. To either side of the window recess are the allegorical figures of Venus chastising Cupid and Summer. The royal arms, supported by a lion and dragon, are sculpted into the frieze over the fireplace. In planning this room, Bess must have at least hoped for a visit from the Queen. An inventory of the house from 1601 lists portraits of all but one of the Tudor monarchs; there were three portraits of Elizabeth. Sir Christopher Hatton's 'Gideon' tapestries are in the gallery, which is one of the largest in England, not even diminished by the unusually large – nineteen feet high – tapestries. Of the other sets of tapestries purchased from Sir Christopher's nephew William Hatton, the 'Abraham' set was used as an alternative set in the 'Withdrawing Chamber'; the six 'personages' tapestries purchased from Hatton were hung in 1601 in 'My Lady's Withdrawing Chamber' on the first floor. The withdrawing chamber on the second floor, also known as the 'State Withdrawing Room', contains an alabaster overmantel carved with Apollo and the Nine Muses, with the royal arms and the Queen's initials; it was made in the 1570s and came from Chatsworth. Of particular interest in this room is the sensuously designed walnut 'sea dog' table, which is held up by chimeras or sea dogs resting on tortoises. It may have come to Bess as a gift from Elizabeth, for similar beasts can be seen on one of the Queen's chairs depicted in an engraving of 1575.

Though so much care was taken to honour Elizabeth at Hardwick, she never visited Bess's masterpiece, just as she never visited Wollaton or Holdenby. One of the joys, and much of the motivation, in building a great country house in the late sixteenth century was the hope, however faint, that the Queen might one day admire it. Each house – Theobalds, Holdenby, Wollaton, Hardwick and others – represented an individual relationship with Elizabeth. No other period in English domestic architecture has been so personally connected with the monarch. To describe a house as 'Georgian', 'Victorian' or 'Edwardian', conveys a particular style, or styles. To say a house is 'Elizabethan' is far more complex. Theobalds and Holdenby were created specifically as palaces for Elizabeth. Wollaton was an episode in Arthurian legend bundled with Renaissance philosophy. Hardwick was a cross-fertilization of ideas from these and other buildings. In 1662, Thomas Fuller described Holdenby as an 'emblem of human happiness'. This statement could apply to most of the great houses of the era. For a few unique decades, builders attempted to capture exuberance, even paradise, and thus 'allure liking'.

Entertaining a Goddess

See where she comes, see where she comes
With flowery garlands crownèd
Queen of all queens renownèd
Thus sang the shepherds and nymphs of Diana
Long live fair Oriana

(part of a madrigal written by John Bennet from
Triumphs of Oriana, edited by Thomas Morley, 1601)

Above
A genealogical chart painted around 1603, tracing the Tudor roots of Mary Stuart, Queen of Scots, and her son James VI of Scotland and I of England. It now hangs in the 'Long Gallery' at Parham in West Sussex.

Opposite The 'State Withdrawing Room' at Hardwick Hall, showing the walnut 'sea dog' table supported by sea dogs resting on tortoises. The room is lined with sumptuous tapestries, as were most of the house's apartments.

While Queen Elizabeth romanced the public with spectacles of majesty – further promoted by art, music and literature – she was winning her subjects' allegiance. In foreign policy, she flirted and prevaricated her way through potential conflict, striving for neutrality, while building up England's navy and financial resources. Yet it was a series of challenges and crises – both domestic and foreign – that could not be avoided or dissolved by wooing which ultimately galvanized the English people in their loyalty to the Queen, and brought about the cult of Elizabeth.

One figure in the events, Mary Stuart, Queen of Scots, was an inadvertent contributor to Elizabeth's success. The daughter of King James V of Scotland and Mary of Guise, Mary, a Catholic, was only a week old when her father died in 1542, and she was proclaimed Queen of Scots. She was sent to live in France, and at the age of fifteen she married the Dauphin, Francis, son of Henry II and Catherine de' Medici, who later became King Francis II. In 1558, the year of Mary's marriage, Protestant Elizabeth succeeded to the throne of England. Mary immediately claimed the throne for herself on the grounds of Elizabeth's illegitimacy; as the granddaughter of Margaret Tudor (Henry VIII's sister) and James IV of Scotland, she had a justifiable claim, which she flaunted by assuming the style and titles of an English monarch. In 1559, her husband became king of France, but died a year later. Mary had no other choice but to return to Scotland, which had become a Protestant country in her absence. From that moment, the Queen of Scots was the focus of Catholic plots to depose Elizabeth.

In 1569, Elizabeth faced the most serious uprising of her reign – the Northern Rebellion – caused by her predominantly Catholic northern earls, who resented the Queen's religious policy and her interference in their independence; they also distrusted Elizabeth's Principal Secretary of State, William Cecil, Lord Burghley. The rebels – the Percies, the Nevilles and the Dacres – advocated a marriage between the Duke of Norfolk, England's most eminent peer, and the Queen of Scots. They hoped that Norfolk would use his influence to achieve the long-term objective of putting Mary on the English throne. When Elizabeth learned of the proposed marriage, Norfolk was sent to the Tower, and the northern earls immediately revolted. The uprising was quashed, but at considerable cost to England; Elizabeth was unforgiving in her vengeance. She knew who had stirred up all the trouble, and gave the Queen of Scots the synonym by which she has ever since been known: 'The Daughter of Debate'.

Mary, it seems, lacked political judgment. She irritated the powerful Protestant reformer John Knox, a situation not improved by her disastrous marriage in 1565 to her Catholic cousin Henry Stuart, Lord Darnley, by whom she had a son in 1566. The following year, Darnley was murdered, and Mary, along with James Hepburn, 3rd Earl of Bothwell, was suspected of complicity in his death. In 1567, she married Bothwell, and consequently lost many supporters. After a battle against the Scottish lords, Mary was imprisoned and forced to abdicate. Bothwell escaped to Norway, and eventually died in prison in Denmark. Mary's son was declared King James VI of Scotland and was raised a Protestant. In 1568, Mary escaped from prison, was involved in another battle, and having ruined all her chances in Scotland, fled to England where she remained a prisoner, mostly in comfortable surroundings, for nineteen years. Her presence on English soil helped bind the Scottish opponents of Mary to the English side, and, for the first time in history, brought about an alliance between Scotland and England.

As a result of the Northern Rebellion, Elizabeth was declared excommunicate by Pope Pius V in his bull *Regnans in excelsis* of 1570, by which the English people were absolved of their allegiance to the monarch, and Catholic princes were encouraged to invade England. Elizabeth's subjects felt the snub to both their sovereign and their sovereignty; the Pope's edict in fact strengthened Elizabeth's position by encouraging Protestant loyalty, and discouraging Catholicism, the practice of which had become tantamount to disloyalty.

Meanwhile, the Queen of Scots kept herself busy in England with needlework, and in pursuing plots to depose Elizabeth. The Ridolfi plot of 1571

again involved Norfolk, who had been released after the demise of the northern earls. According to the Catholic conspirators' plan – which was supported by Spain – Norfolk was to wed Mary, and make her queen of England. After the conspiracy was discovered, Norfolk was executed; Parliament also demanded the execution of Mary, but Elizabeth refused. The Queen of Scots was involved in two more conspiracies against Elizabeth, one in 1583 and another in 1586; the latter involved a plan for the Queen's murder, after which Elizabeth reluctantly signed a warrant for Mary's execution. The Queen of Scots was beheaded at Fotheringhay Castle, near Peterborough, on 8 February 1587. After Mary's death, Elizabeth stormed with grief and anger, but she had greater cause for joy, for with the removal of the Queen of Scots there was no longer an alternative ruler of England. The country became, at last, united under Elizabeth, and ready as a nation to face the first Battle of Britain – the defeat of the Spanish Armada in the summer of 1588.

Later in 1588, on a cold December evening, Godfrey Goodman, a student, and his companions waited in the dark outside the gates of Somerset House. They had hurried to the spot upon learning that the Queen was inside the building and might be seen on her return to Whitehall Palace. They shivered with cold for one and a half hours until the gates of the forecourt opened and torch-bearers illuminated the way as Elizabeth and her entourage, 'in great state', approached the now crowded street. The people, and the young men with them, knelt down as the Queen came near, and shouted: 'God save your Majesty!' 'God bless you all, my good people!' she answered. They cried again: 'God save your Majesty!' And then turning to the crowd, the Queen spoke: 'Ye may well have a greater prince, but ye shall never have a more loving prince.' Goodman described the scene: 'And so the queen and the crowd [stood] there, looking upon one another awhile, [before] her Majesty departed. This wrought such an

Entertaining a Goddess

Background The state bed which travelled with Elizabeth on her progresses was made of walnut and looked very similar to this sixteenth-century bed in the 'Spangled Bedroom' at Knole in Kent. One set of the Queen's bed-hangings was decorated with gold and silver work, as here, though the posts of Elizabeth's bed were topped with the Queen's beasts and bunches of ostrich feathers spangled with gold.

Opposite The bedchamber at Loseley Hall, known as the 'Queen's Room'. It was occupied on four occasions by Elizabeth when her progresses through the southern counties took her to the Surrey manor house then belonging to Sir William More, one of the Queen's most trusted advisers. In preparation for these visits, the drive leading to the house had to be strewn with straw to avoid jolting Elizabeth in her carriage. Sir William was also to 'avoyde his family', meaning remove them from the house. On one occasion, it was ordered that Loseley had to be cleaner than during the Queen's previous visit.

impression upon us … that all the way long we did nothing but talk what an admirable queen she was and how we would adventure our lives in her service.'

Outside London, Elizabeth showed herself to the people during her summer progresses *en route* to one of her great country houses, or to those of wealthy subjects, where she was cosseted and lavishly entertained. During her reign, she visited Hampshire, Huntingdonshire, Leicestershire, the Midlands, East Anglia, the southern counties, Oxford University, Cambridge University, Bristol, Southampton, Worcester, Warwick and Stafford. There were fewer summer progresses in times of danger – especially in the 1580s – and as she got older. However, in 1600, when she was sixty-seven, she scoffed at her ministers who tried to dissuade her from moving on from Nonsuch in Surrey, remarking that the old and frail could remain behind but the young and fit would accompany her. Along the way, she displayed – as always – the regalia and deportment of a great queen, but one imbued with touching warmth and graciousness.

Beyond the impression made by Elizabeth herself, the magnitude of moving the Queen, the Court and all their provisions across the countryside could not have failed to strike awe in onlookers. Three hundred carts were needed to transport the goods and finery – including Elizabeth's bed and hip-bath – that accompanied these sojourns. Then there were the legions of liveried servants of the Queen and the courtiers, dressed in rich fabrics, and in all colours – crimson, blue, yellow, black, and so on. The lords and ladies were always exquisitely attired, and mounted upon the best horses in England. Elizabeth, it was commented, looked particularly well and in command upon her mount. Occasionally, she journeyed by coach, one of which was drawn by Pomeranian horses with their tails and manes dyed orange. The sides of the coach were left open so that she could be seen by her people. The cavalcade ambled along, moving ten or twelve miles in a day, to the musical accompaniment of tambour, pipe and, at stopping places, cornets and trumpets. All along the route, crowds cheered and hallooed from every vantage point, while jostling for a better look. Then they would fall upon their knees as the Queen passed, cheering her again and again. Sometimes she would stop, spread her arms as if to embrace them all, and say a few kind words to even the meanest of her subjects. She could, said the writer Thomas Churchyard, 'draw the hearts of the people after hyr wheresoever she travels'.

By the mid-1570s, Elizabeth's summer visits had reached legendary status. The momentum of adulation was maintained in the style of entertainments staged for

her pleasure. In August 1575, she made a memorable visit to Sir Henry Lee, her future Master at Arms, at Woodstock in Oxfordshire. In 1571, Lee had become lieutenant of the royal manor of Woodstock, in charge of the park and palace; Elizabeth first visited him there in 1572. It seems she felt little discomfort on returning to her former prison: after becoming queen she visited Woodstock on six occasions. For Elizabeth's visit in 1575, Lee organized a contest between knights for the love of a damsel named Gaudina. The spectacle was dramatized with scenery, speeches and poems. The contenders were Contarenus, whom the lady loved, and Loricus, who had once loved a matchless lady without hope of attaining her, and who now sought to earn a reputation in feats of arms; Loricus was meant to represent Lee. It had been foretold to Contarenus that in seven years time he would be united with his beloved lady, but 'first he should fight with the hardiest knight, and see the worthiest Lady of the world', and that a blind hermit would help him, by doing so recovering his sight. Gaudina and Loricus had been told that they would find contentment when they came to 'a place where men were most strong, women most fayre, the country most fertile, the people most wealthy, the government most just, and the princes most worthy'. The fighting between the two knights commenced, but was soon halted by the intervention of a hermit, and the parties were brought before Elizabeth who stood 'in a fine Bower', covered with ivy, which contained 'seates made of earthe with sweet-smelling hearbes'. Each told the Queen their previous history, and at length the hermit explained that though he was now wrinkled and 'cast into a corner', he had once loved a lady who took on many shapes; eventually she became a tigress, upon which he fled from her. He went to the temple of Venus, where he was stricken blind. Mercury took him to Apollo at Delphos, where he received the consolation that he would recover his sight, but not 'till at one time and in one place, in a countrie of most peace two of the most valiant knights shall meet, and the most virtuous Lady of the world shall be there to looke on'. And in Elizabeth's happy presence the knights fought, the lovers met, and the hermit regained his sight. Loricus goes on to pursue his purpose whose 'end will be reward, at least most reputation, with noblest women most esteemed'.

Thereafter, Elizabeth was led to a banqueting house built on a mound forty feet high. The banqueting house was formed from the bent and twisted branches of an oak, and as the Queen nibbled confections, the sound of music came from a hollow beneath the structure. She was visited by the 'Queen of the

Entertaining a Goddess

Right A portrait of Sir Henry Lee, painted by Antonio Mor in 1568. The spheres on Sir Henry's sleeves were meant to represent celestial orbits, emblems associated with Lee. They may also imply the idealized relationship of courtiers with the Queen: one of satellites orbiting a heavenly body in perfect harmony. The patterning of the sleeves also incorporates lovers' knots, and the gold chains may have been a gift from Elizabeth. The rings – adorning the fingers, tied around an arm, and hanging from a red (the colour of passion) cord – are thought to be connotations of special affection, and the placement of Lee's hand is a gesture of heartfelt faithfulness.

Fayry' who was brought to the place upon a wagon of state drawn by six children. The Fairy Queen, making perhaps her first appearance in Elizabethan literature, recited verses saying that her love for Elizabeth had changed her hue from black into white. She then gave gifts to Elizabeth and her ladies. More verses were recited, and when her visit ended, the Queen was reported to have been greatly pleased with all that she had seen and heard.

Loricus, or rather Sir Henry Lee, eventually took for himself the title of 'Queen's Champion', initiating at Whitehall the Accession Day tilts, which were first recorded in 1581. In the jousts and tournaments, Lee revitalized the Burgundian tradition of chivalry – which had been allowed to wane towards the end of Henry VIII's reign – combining Arthurian legend and Protestant ethos to create an allegorical model in which Elizabeth was worshipped by her knights as the Vestal Virgin of the Reformed Religion. These quasi-religious and political pageants employed scholars, poets, musicians and craftsmen to translate the theme into entertainment. Costumes and props took on as much importance as broken lances and the competitors' prowess on their horses.

Queen Elizabeth's Accession Day had long been celebrated throughout the country with bell-ringing, prayers, bonfires and the firing of guns. After Sir Henry Lee introduced the Accession Day tilts, notice of the event was given by parish ministers from their pulpits, claiming it was a holiday 'which passed all the Pope's holidays'. Everyone was invited to watch the festivities at Whitehall, provided they paid a small entrance fee and occupied the designated public stands, which held several thousand spectators. Eventually, programmes were distributed containing the thematic verses and devices that were to be used in the tilt.

The presentation began at noon when the Queen and her ladies took their seats in the tilt-yard gallery. When she was seated, knights in armour rode into the yard upon pageant cars decorated with allegorical symbols, or on horses. Their servants and horses wore corresponding 'disguises'. As each combatant approached the barrier, he halted beneath the gallery while his squire explained, either in verse or in ludicrous speech designed to make Elizabeth laugh, the meaning of his lord's attire. The squire then presented to Elizabeth the knight's shield painted with the device or *impresa* he bore in the tournament. After each knight had been presented, Elizabeth signalled for the tournament to commence.

The chivalrous ideal was personified by Sir Philip Sidney, who could joust for his queen with the best of them. He had been one of the 'four Foster Children of Desire' making a mock attack upon Elizabeth in her 'Fortresse of Perfect Beautie' during the tilt-yard pageant of 1581. In Sidney's famous prose-romance *Arcadia,* a tournament is enacted between the knights of Iberia and the knights of Corinth, in which Henry Lee, Philip Sidney and Elizabeth are thinly disguised as Lelius, Philisides and Helen, Queen of Corinth. Like the knights of the Accession Day tilts, armour is elaborated with costume in Sidney's work: a Frozen Knight wears armour representing ice; a Shepherd Knight is covered in wool, and accompanied by his servants carrying lances camouflaged as hooked staffs; and there is a Phoenix Knight who bursts into flames, from which he emerges unscathed. In 1586, shortly before his thirty-second birthday, Sir Philip Sidney died after a real battle at Zutphen in Holland. As a final chivalrous gesture, he gave up his water flask to a dying soldier, though in earnest need of it himself. Sidney eventually became the idealized representative of the chivalrous age 'what great Eliza's reign hath bred'. He was remembered in Shelley's *Adonais* – 'Sublimely mild, a Spirit without spot' – and in W B Yeats's 'In Memory of Major Robert Gregory', in which Gregory is compared with Sidney: 'Our Sidney and our perfect man'. During the Accession Day tilt of 1586, after Sidney's death, a riderless horse joined the pageant in remembrance of him. Elizabeth's Accession Day continued to be observed as a public holiday in the schools of Westminster for nearly three hundred years. That Sir Henry Lee began the Accession Day festivities is perhaps not surprising, for he was described as being 'adorned with those flowers of knighthood, courtesy, bounty [and] valour which quickly gave forth their fruit'.

Sir Walter Scott drew upon the life of Sir Henry for his novel *Woodstock,* published in 1826. Before her visit to Woodstock in the summer of 1575, Elizabeth spent nineteen days – the longest visit she was ever to make to a subject – with her 'dear Robin', Sir Robert Dudley, Earl of Leicester, at Kenilworth Castle in Warwickshire. That visit provided the inspiration for Scott's earlier work *Kenilworth,* published in 1821.

Of all Elizabeth's annual progresses, the summer of 1575 was probably the most

Entertaining a Goddess

CÆTERA FAMA~
E D

magical. Her future hosts were strained to equal the delights provided by the Earl of Leicester: he was a stylish, dynamic man, and as Queen Elizabeth's Master of the Horse, an expert at organization and presentation. He also held a special place in Elizabeth's heart, and it was thought that during her visit, Leicester, aided by the romantic setting of Kenilworth, would make a final bid for her hand – a subject of constant speculation since the Queen's earliest days on the throne.

Elizabeth and Leicester had been born in the same year, knew each other as children, and had both enjoyed the tutelage of Roger Ascham. As a young man, Leicester had been imprisoned in the Tower when Elizabeth herself became a prisoner there, and they had each suffered the execution of a parent: Leicester's father, the Duke of Northumberland, had been executed in 1553 for altering the succession in order to put on the throne Lady Jane Grey, the wife of his son Guildford Dudley. Northumberland was buried within the Tower, between Anne Boleyn and Katherine Howard. The Earl of Leicester had been arrested for supporting his father's plan, and sentenced to death, but after a year in prison he was released and pardoned, possibly due to the intervention of Philip II, Queen Mary's husband. During Mary's reign, when Elizabeth was in financial straits, Leicester sold some of his lands to give her money. He said of Elizabeth, 'I have known her better than any man alive since she was eight years old.'

But before his seventeenth birthday in 1550, Leicester – then simply Sir Robert Dudley (he did not become an earl until 1565) – married Amy Robsart, a marriage which William Cecil described as 'begun in passion, ended in mourning'. Elizabeth was present at their wedding. However, she continued to maintain a high regard for her childhood friend, and during the first meeting of her Privy Council at Hatfield in November 1558, she made Leicester – a renowned horseman – her Master of the Horse. With the flourish of a great impresario, he immediately began planning Elizabeth's entry into London. Despite Leicester's marriage, the two were openly affectionate, the cause of endless speculation both in England and abroad on the intimacy of the relationship. It was rumoured that Dudley might soon be free to marry the Queen, for Amy was plagued with 'a malady in one of her breasts'. It was also rumoured that he might not wait for the disease to run its course, and that he might rid himself of his wife by divorce, or even poison. In September 1560, Amy was found dead at the foot of a stone staircase in the house of a family friend. Her neck was broken. Inevitably, she was said to have been murdered.

Above A delicate red-chalk drawing of Elizabeth produced by the Italian artist Federico Zuccaro in 1574 as a preparatory sketch for a full-length portrait, which no longer exists. It has been suggested that this drawing is the Queen's closest likeness.

Leicester had been at Court at the time, and an inquest declared the death accidental. It was also rumoured that Elizabeth may have been implicated. Neither possibility could be supported by the evidence.

The two continued to grow close. It was certainly Leicester's hope that Elizabeth would marry him, and Elizabeth took eager pleasure in talking about the possibility. If she had to marry an Englishman, she said, the Earl of Leicester would be her choice. The more affectionate they became, the more malicious gossip-mongers claimed that the Earl 'hath got the Queen with child'. Yet in 1562, Elizabeth, delirious and believing herself to be on the point of death from smallpox, claimed that although she had always loved Leicester, as God was her witness, nothing improper had passed between them. She also told her Council that if she were to die she wanted Leicester to rule England. He could not be king, but he could, however, be made Lord Protector, becoming *de facto* ruler of the country, as Edward Seymour had done fifteen years earlier. Furthermore, she asked that £500 a year be given to Leicester's body-servant. After Elizabeth recovered, their intimacy continued. The French ambassador claimed that the Queen slept with the Earl on New Year's night of 1566, a rumour not dispelled by Leicester's habit of going into her bedchamber early in the morning and handing Elizabeth her shift.

In 1565, after playing tennis with the Duke of Norfolk, Leicester unthinkingly snatched Elizabeth's handkerchief from her hand to mop the sweat from his brow. The Duke was shocked by this glaring presumption, which eventually led to a division in the Court: Norfolk's followers wore yellow and Leicester's blue. On another occasion, on 30 June, Midsummer's Day, Leicester gave a water party on the Thames for the Queen, and invited the Spanish ambassador to join them on their barge. Leicester and Elizabeth began talking playfully of marriage, and he made the suggestion that since a bishop was on a nearby barge, he should be brought to where they were and marry them there and then. Elizabeth jokingly said she doubted if the clergyman knew enough English to perform the ceremony, at which point the Spanish ambassador entered into the game, proclaiming that if the Queen and Leicester would restore Catholicism to the realm, he himself would be the priest who performed the wedding.

Leicester took every opportunity to pursue his suit. In 1562, he brought the tragedy *Gorboduc*, or *The Tragedy of Ferrex and Porrex* to the Court. The story is based on the legendary history of England by Geoffrey of Monmouth, in which the country falls into civil war and devastation for lack of an heir to the throne.

Above The companion sketch to Zuccaro's drawing of Elizabeth shows the Queen's favourite Sir Robert Dudley, Earl of Leicester, dressed in ceremonial armour ready for the tilt, except he wears a hat instead of a helmet.

Three years later, Leicester brought to Whitehall a play that included a dialogue in which Juno praised marriage and Diana argued for chastity, while Jupiter arbitrated in favour of matrimony. During the play, Elizabeth turned to an ambassador and said: 'This is all against me'.

The following summer, Elizabeth visited Oxford University. As Chancellor of the university, Leicester undoubtedly approved the performance of *Palamon and Arcite* enacted by the students. In the course of the play, a prince and a noble contend for the hand of a beautiful maiden. The noble wins but dies, leaving the girl to marry the socially superior prince. At the time of Elizabeth's visit to Oxford, negotiations were under way for her to marry Archduke Charles of Austria, and thereby secure a Habsburg alliance. Elizabeth had made a half-hearted attempt to create a tie between England and Scotland by proposing the then Sir Robert Dudley as a bridegroom for the Queen of Scots. It was at this point that he actually became the Earl of Leicester. Elizabeth increased his social credentials to make him more acceptable to Mary, though perhaps she betrayed a certain lack of seriousness in her intentions by reaching down and tickling him on the back of the neck during the investiture. A few days after the ceremony, Elizabeth invited Sir James Melville, Mary's representative, to her bedchamber to show him a great ruby and other treasures that she kept locked in a little cabinet. Among the items was a miniature of Leicester wrapped in paper across which Elizabeth had written 'My Lord's picture'. Melville asked if he might send the picture to Mary, but Elizabeth would not part with it. She added that if the Queen of Scots would be ruled by her then she could expect to inherit everything Elizabeth possessed. It seems the Queen of Scots was ruled by her heart, for she soon married Lord Darnley, much to the Earl of Leicester's relief.

In 1574, the popular Italian artist Federico Zuccaro came to England for a few months to work for Elizabeth and Leicester. He painted a pair of full-length portraits of the couple, for which there now exist only the red-chalk drawings. Sir Roy Strong has suggested that Zuccaro's image of Elizabeth represents her nearest likeness. Dressed in the graceful, flowing style of the 1570s, she holds a fan made of feathers. Leicester gave her such a fan in the year of Zuccaro's visit: 'a fan of white feathers set in a handle of gold, the one side thereof garnished with diamonds and rubies; on each side a white bear, and two pearls hanging, a lion ramping with a white muzzled bear at the foot'; a bear was part of Leicester's personal device. Zuccaro portrayed Dudley dressed for the tilt, except he wears a hat instead of a helmet. The particular interest of the full-length portraits is that they were painted as a pair. There are other portraits of Elizabeth supposedly painted by Zuccaro, but in view of his short stay in England it is difficult to know if they are genuine. A charming example exists at Sudeley Castle in Gloucestershire.

Though Leicester enjoyed more freedom with Elizabeth than anyone else, her indomitable will always prevailed. In an argument about one of Leicester's men who was refused entrance to the presence chamber, Elizabeth is said to have screamed: 'God's death, my Lord, I will have here one mistress but no master'. There were many times when Leicester would have to bridle his ego, but the tenderness and love-talk always returned. However, the much desired consummation of his relationship with Elizabeth probably never occurred, and he sought instead the physical charms of other ladies of the Court. His enemies spread the rumour that Leicester would pay handsomely to 'seek pasture among the waiting gentlewomen of Her Majesty's great Chamber'. He had an affair with Lady Frances Howard, and with Lady Douglass Sheffield he had a son. Later, he took up with the Court beauty Lettice Knollys, Countess of Essex. When Lettice's husband died in 1578, the couple were secretly married; weeks later, Lettice gave birth to a son. Each of Leicester's amorous dalliances was deeply wounding to Elizabeth; she expected loyalty from all her courtiers, particularly from him. She would rage, she would weep, but the relationship held, and she would eventually forgive. Thus, they went on. In 1585, John Lyly's play *Endymion, the Man in the Moon* was performed before Elizabeth at Greenwich. In the play, an adaptation of a Greek myth, Endymion, a shepherd, loves the inaccessible Cynthia, goddess of the moon, for whom he has deserted his former earthly love Tellus. A witch casts him into a forty-year spell, from which only a kiss from Cynthia can release him. Tellus is imprisoned but eventually becomes infatuated with her gaoler. Cynthia kisses Endymion and, in acknowledging his faithful love, restores his youth; Cynthia and Endymion represent Elizabeth and Leicester, and Tellus may be Lady Sheffield. Beyond an idealistic love, the play may also portray the suspension of Leicester's favour, and a plea for its restoration.

When Leicester died in 1588, Elizabeth shut herself in her chamber until Lord Burghley ordered the door to be broken down. Fifteen years later, when she herself died, a note written by Leicester was found in a cabinet she kept near her bed. In it he thanked the Queen for some medicine she had sent, and asked 'how my gracious Lady doth'. Across its folded surface, Elizabeth had written

Right One of the several portraits of Elizabeth thought to be by Federico Zuccaro. This work is now held at Sudeley Castle in Gloucestershire.

'His last letter'. In his will, Leicester left to his 'most dear and gracious Sovereign whose creature under God I have been, the jewel with three great emeralds with a fair large table diamond in the middle without a foil and set about with many diamonds without foil and a rope of fair white pearl to the number of six hundred'. She wore the pearls in many of her official portraits, including the *Armada Portrait*.

Leicester had always been generous with his gifts for Elizabeth. His New Year's gifts were variously intimate, practical and purely opulent. Among them were a diamond necklace made of his cinquefoils interspersed with lovers' knots; a white satin doublet fastened with eighteen pairs of gold clasps; a diamond-and-ruby clock; a pair of gold bodkins, set with diamonds and rubies, for her hair; fourteen large and sixteen small buttons engraved with the bear and ragged staff and lovers' knots, and set with diamonds and rubies; a porringer made of bloodstone with gold handles in the form of snakes, and so on. Elizabeth gave to Leicester the customary New Year's gift of plate. She also gave him two former monasteries, a house in Kew, the lordship and castle of Denbigh, estates in more than twenty counties, and the castle and parklands of Kenilworth in Warwickshire. Leicester filled his houses, particularly Kenilworth, and the houses he acquired in Wanstead and London, with luxuries. A great collector of art, he amassed 191 paintings, beautiful tapestries – he invested in a tapestry manufactory – and innumerable objects in gold, silver and Venetian glass. He had a genuine interest in literature, and possessed an impressive library

Above A view
of the ruined
Kenilworth Castle
in Warwickshire,
showing one of the
buildings that
Leicester added.
On the first floor
of the building
were Elizabeth's
apartments, which
included an entrance
chamber, a dining
chamber and a
bedchamber. Above
were the quarters for
her ladies-in-waiting.
The overall design
was Gothic; classical
decorations were
restricted to the
porch and the
fireplaces, which
were embellished
with fluted columns.

of books bound in crimson velvet and stamped with his crest in gold. More
books were dedicated to Leicester than to any other courtier, although to
receive a dedication was not always agreeable: royalties did not yet exist and
the practice became a means for writers to make money. Nevertheless, he was
a keen advocate of men of letters: he introduced Edmund Spenser to the
Queen, and Arthur Golding dedicated his translations of Ovid's *Metamorphoses*
to Leicester, the first four books appearing in 1565, and the completed work
in 1567. It was one of the most popular literary works of the Elizabethan era,
portraying with mythological and historical figures a series of tales beginning
with the creation of the world and ending with the deification of Augustus.
Golding said Leicester was 'wont to encourage [literary men] to proceed in
their painful exercise'.

Elizabeth's greatest gift to her greatest favourite was Kenilworth Castle,
which she presented to Leicester in 1563. Leicester's father, the Duke of
Northumberland, had acquired the castle from the Crown, just three months
before his execution in 1553, after which it again came into the possession of
the Crown. Today in ruins, Kenilworth had been a picturesque fortress of red

Right The gatehouse which Leicester added to Kenilworth Castle. From here, the Queen and her party rode out to join the chase on mornings when hunting was favoured.

sandstone set amid a hundred-acre lake; the lake had been created by damming the 'wild brooks' that poured through the meadows. The oldest parts of the structure were built in the twelfth century. Nearly two hundred years later, John of Gaunt (who in Shakespeare's play *Richard II* speaks the patriotic 'this earth, this realm, this England') remodelled the buildings, creating an exquisite hall and private apartments. Henry V added a lakeside banqueting house which he called *Le Plesaunz en Marys* (the Pleasure House in the Marsh). A hundred years later, Henry VIII constructed a range of lodgings across the building's inner court.

After Leicester received Kenilworth, he set to work spending a fortune, altering and improving his castle in order to convert the fortress into a magnificent palace to delight the Queen. Elizabeth had visited the Earl at Kenilworth before the summer of 1575, and had seen the work in progress. He built a new gatehouse to make an immediate impact upon visitors, added a vast new range of lodgings, and altered the keep. The overall style that Leicester chose for his additions was Gothic, which seems unadventurous for a well-read man who had been to the Continent, and whose father had previously employed John Shute to gather knowledge of Italian classical architecture; Shute's book *The First and Chief Groundes of Architecture* was published in the same year that Leicester acquired Kenilworth. But instead of being examples of bold classicism, the Earl of Leicester's additions enhanced the Gothic structure of Kenilworth, creating a chivalrous, enchanted-castle backdrop that was perfectly in keeping with the entertainments planned for the Queen's visit in 1575. He did, however, acknowledge the classical style in the design of the porch – later added to the gatehouse – with its door set into a rounded arch flanked by twin sets of pilasters with shell-topped niches; inside the gatehouse, a fireplace and overmantel are decorated with pilasters and columns. Both porch and overmantel were probably transferred from Leicester's other buildings, and with their survival they give an indication of the grandeur of his additions. The new buildings had very large windows, which apparently impressed Robert Laneham, who as well as being the Council Porter, in charge of guarding entry to the Council Chamber, was also in Leicester's service. In a letter he wrote to his friend Humphrey Martin, narrating Leicester's entertainments for the Queen in 1575, Laneham described his impressions of the house:

A day tyme, on every syde so glittering by glasse; a nights, by continuall brightnesse of candel, fyre and torchlight, transparent throogh the lyghtsom wyndz [windows], az it wear [were] the

Opposite The carefully laid-out gardens of present-day Kenilworth Castle. As they appear here, the gardens in Elizabeth's day were divided into quarters and separated by grass walks edged with sand.

Egiptian Pharos relucent [shimmering] untoo all the Alexandrian coast: or els … thus radiaunt az thoogh Phoebus [here meaning Apollo, the god of the sun] for hiz eaz woold rest him in the Castl, and not every night so travell dooun unto the Antipodes.

Leicester paid great attention to the interior of the house, too. From the inventory of Kenilworth we know, for example, that the furniture in the apartments, added especially for Elizabeth's visit, was upholstered with a silvery material in shades of peach, purple and crimson.

Leicester's garden at Kenilworth occupied an acre to the north of the castle, along which ran a grass terrace walk ten feet high and twelve feet broad, interspersed with the obelisks and decorative white bears and staffs forming Leicester's badge. At each end were arbours of trees and flowers. In the centre of the walk was an aviary twenty feet high, thirty feet long and fourteen broad. The cage was inset with wire-mesh windows in the shape of arches and flanked by columns. The outside of the cage was painted and gilded to represent diamonds, emeralds, rubies and sapphires. Below the terrace, the garden was divided into quarters, separated by grass walks edged with sand. In the midst of each quarter was an obelisk topped with an orb hewn from porphyry, and surrounded by fragrant herbs, flowers, and apple, pear and cherry trees. The garden walk met at a marble fountain composed of two athletes standing back to back and holding up a ball that spouted water into the basin below, which was stocked with a variety of fish – carp, tench, bream, perch, eel, all 'pleasantly playing'.

Two clock dials were set aloft the battlemented towers of the keep. One clock faced east, the other south; both had gilded numbers 'glittering conspicuously a great way off'. Leicester had the clock stopped at two, the hour, according to Laneham, to take cheer, to see and be seen, and to do honour to the Queen. Laneham also suggested that the number two may have meant Elizabeth and Leicester, as in 'tooz, payrz and cooplz'.

Entertaining a Goddess

Opposite A nineteenth-century sideboard carved from a great oak from the grounds of Kenilworth Castle. Produced for the Great Exhibition of 1851, the sideboard, or buffet, is decorated with scenes of Elizabeth's stay at Kenilworth in 1575. The buffet is at Warwick Castle.

Below A State saddle of the late sixteenth century which may have belonged to Elizabeth. The velvet saddle is at Warwick Castle, once the home of the Earl of Leicester's brother Ambrose Dudley, Earl of Warwick. Elizabeth had stayed at the castle on her way to Kenilworth in 1575.

On the journey to Kenilworth, Elizabeth made a visit to Warwick Castle, where she was a guest of Leicester's brother Ambrose Dudley, Earl of Warwick, and his wife. The dense woods around Warwick were kept well stocked for the Queen's sport. A dainty saddle that may have once belonged to Elizabeth is still at the castle today. It is covered in velvet, now faded grey-blue, but originally emerald-green and embroidered with silver thread. During an earlier visit to Warwick in 1572, the festivities included a mock battle involving flying dragons spewing fireballs across the sky which accidentally set houses ablaze. The house in which two poor unfortunates – Henry Cowy and his wife – had been sleeping burned to the ground. Happily, the couple escaped unharmed, save the loss of their possessions, for which they received £25 donated from the Court. The excitement of Warwick was a gentle overture to the more sensational delights of Kenilworth Castle in 1575. The Queen's visit to Kenilworth is commemorated in an enormous sideboard built by Warwickshire craftsmen in the nineteenth century. The sideboard – now at Warwick Castle – was fashioned from an oak tree felled in the grounds of Kenilworth. It is carved with scenes of Leicester's entertainments for Elizabeth and was made for the Great Exhibition of 1851.

According to Laneham's account, when Elizabeth made her public arrival at Kenilworth, she was first welcomed by one of ten sybils clothed in white silk. At the tilt-yard, a giant, 'full of passions', skulking to and fro, and brandishing a club and keys, was reduced to wonder upon seeing 'a personage so evidently expressing an heroicall Soveraintee over all the whole estates'. He gave up his club, keys, office and all, and on his knees humbly prayed pardon for his ignorance and impatience. Having received Her Majesty's pardon, the giant signalled to his six trumpeters. These were in fact pasteboard trumpeters eight foot tall, bearing silver trumpets five feet long, behind which real men blew trumpets 'very delectably' as Elizabeth rode along the tilt-yard and into the inner gate leading to the centre of the castle. Here, she was greeted by the Lady of the Lake, who stood with her nymphs upon a moving island, the whole assembly illuminated by torchlight and floating towards the shore as Elizabeth approached. The Lady explained that she had kept possession of the lake since King Arthur's days, but upon hearing of the Queen's 'hither cumming' thought

Below
A reconstructed drawing portrays the scene as Elizabeth on horseback makes her public entrance at Kenilworth Castle in 1575, greeted by the Earl of Leicester.

Entertaining a Goddess

it her duty to offer it up and her power therein. The tableau was concluded with the music of oboes, shawms (medieval wind instruments) and cornets.

Elizabeth then came to a bridge seventy feet in length and twenty feet wide with side rails and seven pairs of posts. On the first set of posts were caged birds, meant to be a present from Sylvanus, the god of the woods and fowl. Resting on the second set of posts were large silver bowls filled with apples, pears, cherries, filberts, walnuts, oranges, pomegranates, lemons and pippins, all gifts from Pomona, the goddess of fruits. The third pair of posts supported silver bowls containing wheat, barley, oats, beans and peas from Ceres, the goddess of crops. The fourth pair of posts held on one side a silver bowl brimming with clusters of red and white grapes, and on the other side pots of wine and two glasses 'of good capacitie filld full', one with white wine and the other with claret, presents from Bacchus, the god of wine. On top of the fifth set of posts were large trays heaped with eels, turbot, mullet, herring, oysters, salmon and crayfish from Neptune, the god of the sea. The sixth set of posts bore two ragged staves of silver, and arrows, spears, shields and other armour from Mars, the god of war. On the seventh set of posts were displayed musical instruments – lutes, viols, shawms, cornets, flutes, recorders and harps from Phoebus, the god of music. As Elizabeth crossed the bridge, she was accompanied by a poet dressed in sky-blue and wearing a bay garland upon his head. He pointed out each of the gifts from the gods as they passed, and at the end of the bridge the Queen was received with a 'fresh delicate armony of Flutz'. Passing into the inner court, Elizabeth was helped down from her palfrey and accompanied up to her chamber. Afterwards, there followed a great peal of guns and fireworks, the noise and flames of which could be heard and seen twenty miles off: a gift from Jupiter. Thus ended the first evening's entertainment.

The following days brought music, dancing, hunting, bear-baiting, acrobats, a country wedding, an 'ambrosiall' banquet, masques, plays and more fireworks. Regardless of the festivities, the business of the Court pressed on. Five gentlemen were knighted, and Elizabeth touched nine people for the 'evil' scrofula, which was thought to be cured by the sovereign's touch upon the sores and swellings of the afflicted. The highlight of the Kenilworth entertainments was a water pageant, which commenced with Neptune blowing upon his sea-shell trumpet when Elizabeth came near – the god's 'blaster'. The Lady of the Lake made another appearance, with her nymphs and floating island, and they were joined in the lake by an eighteen-foot mermaid, an evil knight and Arion

– the Greek poet and musician of Lesbos – astride a dolphin twenty-four feet in length. Arion sang 'a delectabl ditty' to the accompaniment of six musicians concealed within the dolphin's belly, 'the hole armony conveyed in tyme, tune, & temper … incomparably melodious'.

Throughout the Queen's visit, crowds swarmed the castle in the hope of seeing celebrities and some of the magic. John Shakespeare, an important municipal officer from Stratford-upon-Avon, and his eleven-year-old son William, may have been among the throng, though perhaps John's status allowed the two the privilege of a closer look. If so, the enchantment may have inspired Oberon's speech in *A Midsummer Night's Dream* in which he declares:

Since once I sat upon a promontory
And heard a mermaid on a dolphin's back
Uttering such dulcet and harmonious breath
That the rude sea grew civil at her song.

Elizabeth was guest of honour at the Earl of Derby's marriage to Burghley's granddaughter Lady Elizabeth Vere in 1594, at which the first production of *A Midsummer Night's Dream* was reputedly staged for the Queen's entertainment.

The author of the Kenilworth entertainments was George Gascoigne. Leicester employed him to use his skill with words, costume and scenery to support an overall theme: that Elizabeth should give up her single state, which her subjects and the gods desired, and marry the Earl of Leicester. Even as the Queen departed from Kenilworth Castle, Gascoigne rode beside her, making farewell speeches intermingled with dramatization. He was dressed as Sylvanus, god of the woods, and as they rode along he unravelled a tale about one of Diana's nymphs called Ahtebasile (meaning Elizabeth), and Deepe Desire (Leicester). Deepe Desire had been changed into a holly bush. As the story was told, the party approached a holly bush out of which emerged Deepe Desire, now happily returned to human form. He beseeched Elizabeth to prolong her stay at Kenilworth:

Live here, good Queen, live here; you are amongst your friends;
their comfort comes when you approach, and when you part it ends.

George Gascoigne continued in song, accompanied by music, and finally finished the drama with:

Oh farewell life, delightful death, farewell.
I die in heaven, yet live in darksome hell.

All the same, Elizabeth rode on.

After a short stay at Woodstock, the Queen's progress extended to Berkeley Castle in Gloucestershire, where Leicester suggested the company take advantage of the hunting. Leicester had been engaged in an acrimonious lawsuit with Henry, Lord Berkeley, over the rights to the land surrounding the castle. It was Leicester's view that the land was jointly owned by himself and his brother, devolving from the claim of an ancestor. Lord Berkeley was absent at the time of the Queen's visit, but later, having learned of the matter, and having discovered that the party had helped themselves to twenty-seven of his deer, he considered it something of an invasion. For the Queen's part, she felt that Berkeley should have been glad that she had amused herself in his park, and was infuriated by his attitude. A bedspread thought to have belonged to Elizabeth, and forgotten by her when she left, still remains at Berkeley Castle. It is an exquisite piece of needlework embroidered with pink, white and red flowers against a cream-and-green background.

A month before his death in 1588, the Earl of Leicester stage-managed one of the greatest performances in British history: Elizabeth's speech to her troops at Tilbury in Essex on the eve of the threatened Spanish invasion. Elizabeth had struggled for thirty years to maintain peace, but when conflict finally became unavoidable, she threw all her energy into war, declaring that she would meet the enemy face to face, riding at the head of her army – a proposal the Privy Council would not countenance. The Earl of Leicester wrote to Elizabeth:

… your person being the most dainty and sacred thing we have in this world to care for, a man must tremble when he thinks of it; specially finding your Majesty to have the princely courage to transport yourself to the utmost confines of your realm to meet your enemies and to defend your subjects. I cannot, most dear Queen, consent to that, for upon your well-doing consists all the safety of your whole kingdom and therefore preserve that above all.

Below Elizabeth on horseback during the Kenilworth entertainments in 1575, a detail from the nineteenth-century carved sideboard at Warwick Castle.

Leicester had another plan. Knowing full well the profound emotional response Elizabeth evoked in her subjects, he suggested that she review the troops at Tilbury to raise their morale and fortify their courage for battle.

Elizabeth arrived by river on 8 August 1588. As her barge approached the shore, guns were discharged, and fifes and drums sounded; across the camp, the companies' ensigns were raised as Elizabeth stepped onto the land. A causeway had been prepared and an open coach brought to take her to the middle of the camp. The coach was painted and gilded 'chequerwise', creating the appearance of emeralds, diamonds and rubies. In the camp, Sir Roger Williams, a captain in the Queen's army, met Elizabeth with two thousand horse. He ordered one thousand to lead the Queen's coach and the other thousand to follow, escorting her to Arden Hall, 'a proper, sweet cleanly house' where she was to stay the night. As the Queen's coach moved forward, the ranks, most of whom could see nothing, kept up a continuous shout: 'God save the Queen!' Others fell on their knees. The coach paused, and Elizabeth commanded the soldiers to stand, then she wept as she beheld the men who were ready to die for her.

The next morning, Elizabeth returned to the camp to review the troops. For part of the ceremony she walked through the lines, 'sometimes like a woman, sometimes with the countenance and pace of a soldier'. She then mounted a white horse with dappled grey hindquarters, a gift from Sir Robert Cecil. A breastplate had been found for her to wear, since some members of the Council were concerned she ran a risk going about the camp unprotected. The armour was fastened over her bodice and it shone like silver between the lace ruff and the skirts of her gown. The Earl of Ormonde walked in front of the Queen, carrying the Sword of State. 'Then came the Queen on prancing steed attired like and angel bright.' Lord Leicester walked at her bridle; a page followed, carrying on a cushion a helmet with a white plume. The response from the soldiers was such that 'the earth and air did sound like thunder'. After reviewing the troops, and riding more than a mile, Elizabeth gave her speech:

My loving People, we have been perswaded by some that are careful of our Safety, to take heed how we commit our Self to armed Multitudes, for fear of Treachery; but I assure you, I do not desire to live to distrust my faithful and loving People. Let Tyrants fear, I have always so behaved my self, that under God, I have placed my chiefest Strength and Safeguard in the loyal Hearts and good Will of my Subjects, and therefore I am come amongst you, as you see, at that time, not for my Recreation and Disport, but being resolved, in the midst and heat of

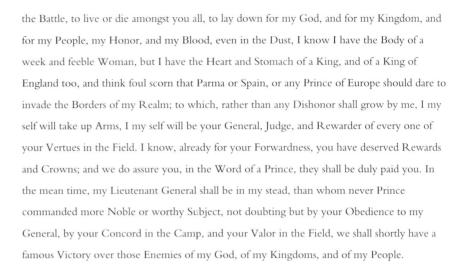

Below An
anonymous panel
painting records the
scene as Elizabeth
reviews her troops at
Tilbury in August
1588. 'Her presence
and her words
fortified the courage
of the captains and
the soldiers beyond
all belief.'

the Battle, to live or die amongst you all, to lay down for my God, and for my Kingdom, and
for my People, my Honor, and my Blood, even in the Dust, I know I have the Body of a
week and feeble Woman, but I have the Heart and Stomach of a King, and of a King of
England too, and think foul scorn that Parma or Spain, or any Prince of Europe should dare to
invade the Borders of my Realm; to which, rather than any Dishonor shall grow by me, I my
self will take up Arms, I my self will be your General, Judge, and Rewarder of every one of
your Vertues in the Field. I know, already for your Forwardness, you have deserved Rewards
and Crowns; and we do assure you, in the Word of a Prince, they shall be duly paid you. In
the mean time, my Lieutenant General shall be in my stead, than whom never Prince
commanded more Noble or worthy Subject, not doubting but by your Obedience to my
General, by your Concord in the Camp, and your Valor in the Field, we shall shortly have a
famous Victory over those Enemies of my God, of my Kingdoms, and of my People.

It was the last progress Elizabeth and Leicester made together.

With each year of Elizabeth's reign, her subjects seemed to compete in
providing imaginative amusements and entertainments. Sir Francis Carew of
Beddington in Surrey, believing Elizabeth had a penchant for cherries, and
anticipating a visit from her after the season, covered his cherry trees
with canvas tents on which he scooped water as 'the heat of the weather
required', in order to retard the ripening of the fruit. Upon being
assured of Her Majesty's visit, Sir Francis removed the tents and 'a few
sunny days' brought the fruit to a 'perfect cherry colour'. In Suffolk, the
Queen was greeted by two hundred young men clothed in white
velvet, and in Bisham in Buckinghamshire, as Elizabeth's entourage
approached the home of Lady Russell, they witnessed two nymphs
(Lady Russell's daughters) repelling the advances of a wanton Pan.
In Hampshire, Edward Seymour, Earl of Hertford, attempted to
recapture some of Kenilworth's fantasy in the water pageant he
planned for Elizabeth's entertainment during the three days she visited
Elvetham in September 1591. Before her arrival, three hundred men
set to work enlarging the house, and on a hillside 'fourteene score off
from the house', they built a room of estate for the nobles and a
withdrawing room for the Queen. The outsides of the walls were
covered with boughs and clusters of ripe hazelnuts, and the insides
with tapestries; the floor was scattered with 'sweet herbs and green
rushes'. Nearby, kitchens and a range of domestic offices were built,

Opposite An
exterior detail of the
present-day Elvetham
Hall in Hampshire, a
remarkable example
of Victorian Gothic
architecture built in
the 1860s.

and a large hall for the entertainment of 'knights, ladies and gentlemen of chiefe account'. Between these buildings and Lord Hertford's house, the workers cut into the earth a great pond in the shape of a crescent moon. In the pond, they made three islands. The first island was fashioned in the form of a ship, a hundred feet long by forty feet broad, bearing three trees representing three masts. The second island took the form of a fort, forty feet square and overgrown with willows. The third was a 'Snayle Mount' (so called for its shape and gradual assent), which rose to four circles of hedges; the whole structure was twenty feet high by forty feet broad. In the water were a variety of boats equipped for music, and a pinnace, or warship, furnished with masts, yards, sails, anchors, cables and 'all the other ordinarie tackling', and decorated with flags, streamers and pendants painted with 'diverse colours and sundry devises'. Lord Hertford was anxious that his efforts would prove a success with Elizabeth and thereby restore him to her favour. He had been out of favour since 1560 for secretly marrying Catherine Grey, sister of Jane Grey, and a potential claimant to the throne. For his crime he was fined £15,000 and imprisoned in the Tower for nine years. His wife was also sent to the Tower, but was later moved, without her husband, to a private house, where she died in 1568.

On the first day, Elizabeth was met two miles from Elvetham by Lord Hertford and his train of three hundred men wearing 'chains of gold about their necks, and in their hats yellow and black feathers'. Upon reaching Elvetham, Elizabeth was welcomed by a poet 'clad in greene, to signify the joy of his thoughts at her entrance'. While the poet spoke his verses complimenting the Queen, whom he said resembled 'some great Goddesse, and whose beames Doe sprinkle Heaven with unacquainted light', six virgins were busily removing blocks from Elizabeth's path; the obstructions had supposedly been laid there by 'Envie'. After the oration, the six virgins walked on before the Queen, strewing the way with flowers, while singing a song with the refrain:

O beauteous Quene of second Troy
Accept of our unfained joy.

The author of the Elvetham entertainments was probably John Lyly.

After supper, the Queen 'graciously admitted unto her presence a notable consort of six musicians ... Their musicke so highly pleased her, that in grace and favour thereof, she gave a newe name unto one of their Pavans, made long since by master Thomas Morley, then organist of Pauls Church.' Being an

accomplished musician on the lute and virginals, Elizabeth
had not only a fondness for music, which was well known,
but also an intellectual appreciation of the work of other
musicians and composers. She had at least sixty musicians in
her service, including the singers of the Chapel Royal and the
instrumentalists of the 'Queen's Musick'. In 1601, Thomas
Morley, not only an organist, but also a madrigalist, edited
Triumphs of Oriana, which celebrated in music the victories of
Elizabeth over her enemies, and in which more than twenty
leading composers and amateurs joined together to honour
the Queen. Each of the set verses ended with:

Then sang the Shepherds and Nymphs of Diana
Long live fair Oriana

In 1592, Thomas Morley had become an organist to the
Chapel Royal, following Thomas Tallis and William Byrd,
Morley's teacher. John Bull had been made organist to the
Chapel Royal in 1591, the year of Queen Elizabeth's visit to
Elvetham. The second half of the sixteenth century was one
of the most distinguished periods in the entire history of English music.

On her second day at Elvetham, Elizabeth viewed the water pageants from a
throne near the crescent-shaped pond. She sat beneath a canopy of estate, made
under Lord Hertford's instructions of green satin lined with green silk, 'everie
seam covered with a broad silver lace; valanced about and fringed with greene
silke and silver', supported with four silver pillows, and topped 'with four white
plumes, spangled with silver'. She watched as sea creatures swam and waded
breast-high in the water. There was Nereus, the prophet of the sea, attired in red
silk with a 'cornerd-cappe' upon his curled head; and five Tritons, with 'grislie
heades' and beards of 'divers colours and fashions', all 'cheerfully sounding their
trumpets'. After them went Neptune and Oceanus, leading the warship wherein
three virgins with cornets played 'Scottish gigs'. With them in the warship
was the sea nymph Neaera, the old love of Sylvanus, god of the woods. The
warship also carried two jewels – presents for Elizabeth. Next to Neaera were
singers, whose song was accompanied by a lute and echoed by singers in another
boat. As the singers sang from one group to the other, the fort was being
surrounded with armed men and the 'Snayle Mount' was made to resemble a

Entertaining a Goddess

'monster having hornes full of wildfire, continually burning'. Against this background of activity, Nereus made an oration to 'Faire Cinthia, the wide Ocean's Empresse'; the jewels were delivered to the Queen, and this was followed by more songs. Sylvanus then made his appearance clad in 'kiddes skinnes with the haire on; his legges, bodie and face [were] naked but died over with saffron, and his head hooded with a goates skin, and two little hornes over his forehead; [and he was] bearing in his right hand an olive tree and in his left a holly scutcheon', on which Apollo had written Elizabeth's praises. Sylvanus spoke verses 'to honour her whom all the world adores', after which he was cast into the pond, instigating a battle between the creatures of the land and the creatures of the sea. Neaera brought the pageant to a close with:

O live in endless joy, with glorious fame
Sound trumpets, sound, in honor of her name.

The following day, Elizabeth was presented with a glorious banquet, preceded by a peal of ordnance discharged from the ship-isle, on which was erected a 'castle of fireworks of all sorts', answered by a 'globe of all manner of fireworks' on the 'Snayle Mount'. To these were added 'running rockets', 'fire-wheeles', 'pikes of pleasure', and 'balles of wilde fire'. In a 'lowe gallerie' in the privy garden, the banquet was served by two hundred of Hertford's men, each carrying so many glasses and silver dishes that the size of the dinner service amounted to a thousand pieces. Their way was lit by a hundred torch-bearers. Among the items of confectionery was a menagerie sculpted in 'sugar-worke'. There was the Queen's coat of arms, and those of her nobles, plus sugar figures of men, women, castles, forts, weapons, drummers, trumpeters, soldiers, mermaids and unicorns, and every kind of animal, reptile, bird and fish, including camels, lions, cranes, frogs, snakes, dolphins and even periwinkles. In addition, there was a variety of fruits, preserves, jellies, marmalades and comfits.

On the day of Elizabeth's departure from Elvetham, the now customary Fairy Queen made a speech. Afterwards, she danced and sang to the accompaniment of an 'exquisite consort' of music played on a lute, a bandora [a stringed instrument similar to a lute], a base-viol, a cittern [another lutelike instrument], a treble-viol and a flute'. The fairies sang:

Elisa is the fairest Quene
That ever trod upon this greene.

Right The present Elvetham Hall, built on the site of the Earl of Hertford's country manor which Elizabeth visited in September 1591.

Elisaes eyes are blessed starres
Inducing peace, subduing warres.

O blessed be each day and hour
Where sweet Elisa builds her bower.

The song and music so delighted Elizabeth that she had it performed twice over. An hour later, as she made her departure, all the sea creatures were in the pond wringing their hands and showing signs of sorrow. Sylvanus was similarly dejected. As Elizabeth passed through the park, music was heard coming from a hidden bower in the woods, and voices sang:

O come againe, sweet beauties sunne:
When thou art gone, our joyes are done

The Queen was greatly pleased with Lord Hertford's hospitality and told him that 'hereafter hee shoulde finde the rewarde thereof in her especiall favour'.

The enchantment of those three September days was later absorbed in the Victorian Gothic architecture of the present Elvetham Hall. It is a contorted mixture of madness and beauty which was built in the 1860s with five additions this century. Inside the house, the drawing room's fireplace portrays Elizabeth being greeted by Lord Hertford in 1591. The painted ceiling in the drawing room depicts characters from Sir Walter Scott's *Kenilworth*. An aerial view of the land near the present-day Elvetham Hall reveals a large depression in the earth – in the shape of a crescent moon.

An interesting side-note to Elizabeth's summer progresses occurred in 1578, during her visit to Melford Hall in Suffolk, then the home of Sir William Cordell, Master of the Rolls. At Melford Hall, the Queen was joined by Monsieur de Bacqueville, another of the Duke of Alençon's envoys who had come to court Elizabeth on his master's behalf. When dining with Bacqueville, the Queen indicated that the gold and silver plate piled high on the sideboards and on the table was not extensive or opulent enough to impress the Frenchman. The plate had been brought on progress from London. The Lord Chamberlain protested that he had never known so much plate carried as that which had accompanied the Queen to Melford Hall. But Elizabeth had no interest in the Lord Chamberlain's views, and in the end more plate was ordered from London. The gold and silver jewel-encrusted salt-cellars, ewers, cups,

Left Melford Hall in Suffolk, which Elizabeth visited during her summer progress of 1578. The owner of the house, Sir William Cordell, Master of the Rolls, altered its design to form an E-plan in honour of the Queen.

Opposite The
banqueting pavilion
at Melford Hall,
where in the upper
storey the Queen
may have nibbled
confections with
Monsieur de
Bacqueville, one of
the Duke of
Alençon's envoys, in
1578. The sash
windows visible here
are an eighteenth-
century addition.

Below The carved
fireplace in the
drawing room of the
present Elvetham
Hall, portraying
Elizabeth being
greeted by the Earl of
Hertford in 1591.

bowls and platters that made up the royal collection were indeed impressive. The additional items displayed during dinner at the next house on the Queen's schedule, Lawshall Hall, also in Suffolk, must have been truly magnificent. Sir William Cordell's parting gifts to Elizabeth were timely: 'A cup of golde, the cover and foote enamuled with eight course diamonds and in the top of the cover a fair emeraude and another cup of golde enameled like thother emerald.' Sir William further honoured Elizabeth in the design of Melford Hall, which had been built around the four sides of a courtyard. He subsequently removed one side to create an E-plan.

On 17 November 1590, Sir Henry Lee staged one of his most magnificent Accession Day tilts in the tilt-yard at Whitehall. That year, 'being by age overtaken', he resigned his post as the Queen's Champion to George Clifford, 3rd Earl of Cumberland. George Peele gave an account of the tilt in his poem *Polyhymia*. At the head of the knights was Sir Henry Lee:

Mighty in arms, mounted on a puissant horse,

Knight of the crown, in rich embroidery

And costly fair caparison charged with crowns

O'ershadowed with a wither'd running vine …

Cumberland was clad in silver armour and white plumes. Among the twelve or fourteen couples that tilted on that day, each was imaginatively dressed. Lord Compton and his men wore white – 'the virgin's colours' – while the Earl of Essex wore black plumes and armour, his attendants dressed in mourning;

Above George Clifford, 3rd Earl of Cumberland, as the Queen's Champion, painted by Nicholas Hilliard. Cumberland wears the costume of the Knight of Pendragon over his star-patterned armour. As the Knight, he came riding into the tilt-yard upon a mock dragon laden with treasure. At the right of the painting, Cumberland's emblematic shield is suspended from a tree. The motto on the shield proclaims that the Earl will use his lance to defend the Queen's honour until the sun, moon and earth are eclipsed.

Sir Charles Blount, 'beset with the glorious sunshine of his train', came as the Sun. After the joust, Lee and Cumberland dismounted and approached the Queen, who sat in the gallery window overlooking the tilt-yard. As they came near, music 'sweete and secrete' was heard, while the earth seemed to open and a 'pavilion' like the sacred Temple of the Virgins Vestal appeared. The temple was made of white taffeta; inside burned many lamps, and on an altar covered with gold, two wax candles 'in rich candlesticks' burned. Next to the candles were princely gifts, which were presented to her Majesty by three virgins. Before the door of the temple stood a crowned pillar embraced by an eglantine tree. Hanging from the tree was a table, upon which was written in gold a prayer to 'Elizae'. The presents and prayer having been delivered, Sir Henry took off his armour, and kneeling, gave it to Cumberland. He then humbly beseeched Elizabeth to accept the Earl for her Champion.

Whereat she smiles, and sighs, and seem'd to say,
'Good woodman, though thy green be turn'd to grey
Have thy request; we take him at thy praise:
May he succeed to the honour of thy days.'

Henry Lee then put on a coat of black velvet, and covered his head with a cap of the country fashion. The new Champion issued a challenge against all comers to take place on 19 November, Saint Elizabeth's Day, which had been inaugurated after the defeat of the Spanish Armada in 1588.

Verses sung during the 1590 Accession Day tilt appear in John Dowland's *First Book of Airs*, published in 1597. The lyrics, though anonymous, may be Lee's own. His authorship is acknowledged in another piece, also set to music by John Dowland, but recorded in Robert Dowland's *A Musical Banquet* of 1610:

Entertaining a Goddess

But ah poore Knight though thus in dreame he ranged
Hoping to serve this Saint in sort most meete,
Tyme with his golden locks to silver changed
Hath with age – fetters bound him hands and feete,
Ay mee, hee cryes, Goddesse my limbs grow faint,
Though I times prisoner be, be you my Saint.

In 1592, two years after his resignation as the Queen's Champion, Sir Henry Lee had one more opportunity to entertain Elizabeth, during her visit to Woodstock. In probably the last drama held at Ditchley, Lee's home situated a few miles from Woodstock, the 'owld Knight' is 'nowe a new religious hermite'. He had previously been Loricus, whose yearly jousts, hymns, songs and emblems were dedicated to the Queen's honour. Now cut off from the Court, he keeps 'a verie courte in his own bosome, making presence of her in his soule, who was absent from his sight'. Loricus falls ill and sends to Elizabeth his last will and testament, recommending to others to serve as he had served. But as the Queen approaches, the dying man makes a miraculous recovery and reads, as a supplement to the will, his legacy: 'the whole Manor of Love'.

Background A sixteenth-century drawing showing knights in armour taking part in a tilt. Dignitaries look down on the scene in the tilt-yard from the gallery window.

Epilogue

Lord Burghley, who had worked with Elizabeth for forty years, said that she 'was the wisest woman that ever was, for she understood the interests and dispositions of all the princes in her time, and was so perfect in the knowledge of her own realm, that no councillor she had could tell her anything she did not know before'. His son Sir Robert Cecil, who after Burghley's death eventually replaced him as Secretary of State, experienced a different relationship with the Queen. In his estimate, 'She was more than a man, and in troth, sometimes less than a woman.' He was cautious in his dealings with Elizabeth, and detached enough to expedite, as early as 1601, a secret correspondence with the preferred incumbent to the English throne, James VI of Scotland, thus laying in credit against the Queen's death. Elizabeth's own correspondence with the Queen of Scots's son – whom she called 'dear Brother' – was, over the years, full of instruction on the attributes becoming a king, and advice on the governance of his realm. She never openly declared in her letters that James would be the next ruler of England, but used instead veiled phrases and obscure language to imply that he would succeed her, leaving the matter not quite settled: she was holding on to her power until the very end.

On the afternoon of 30 November 1601, Elizabeth delivered a speech to 140 members of the House of Commons, who had crowded into the presence chamber of Whitehall Palace. She spoke to the kneeling men for some time, then – out of sympathy for their discomfort – urged them to stand. Towards the end of the oration she concluded:

There will never Queen sit in my seat with more zeal to my country, care to my subjects, and that will sooner with willingness venture her life for your good and safety than myself. For it is my desire to live nor reign no longer than my life and reign shall be for your good. And though you have had, and may have, many princes more mighty and wise sitting in this seat, yet you never had nor shall have, any that will be more careful and loving.

Nearly three weeks later, at the close of what was to be Elizabeth's last parliament, she delivered a speech setting forth her observations of her entire reign. She talked of the Northern Rebellion, and of the attempts upon her life, which God had chosen to spare, 'making me an instrument of his holy will in delivering the state from danger and myself from dishonour'. On foreign policy and the Spanish Armada, she remarked, 'I never gave just cause of war to any prince … nor had any greater ambition than to maintain my own state in security and peace … even that potent Prince, the King of Spain that hath so many ways assailed both my realm and me had many provocations of kindness by my just proceedings'. She also spoke of the ongoing rebellion in Ireland led by Hugh O'Neill, 2nd Earl of Tyrone, who, with the aid of the Spanish army, sought his country's independence. Philip II died in 1598, and his son, Philip III, had taken up the quarrel with England. If the Spanish forces prevailed in Ireland, an invasion of England was anticipated, in preparation for which Parliament had granted subsidies. Elizabeth thanked them for the funds, which, 'like rivers coming from the ocean', would 'return to the ocean again'. As it happened, by the end of the month England was victorious. In this last speech, the Queen said not a word about the subject that had confronted her, and the country, for nearly forty-four years: the succession.

In 1602, her sixty-ninth year, Elizabeth was still in remarkably good health. She rode on horseback ten miles in a single day, and danced till all hours, though after periods of exercise she would seek solitude to conceal her weariness. In September, a foreign visitor to the Court reported that she was never 'so set upon jollity', and on 17 November she celebrated the forty-fourth anniversary of her accession 'with as great an applause of multitudes as if they had never seen her before'. But a month later, Elizabeth was clearly unwell. Sir John Harington, her godson, was saddened at seeing her during Christmas. 'Our dear Queen', he wrote to his wife, 'doth now bear show of human infirmity; too fast for that evil which we

Below A tin plate honouring Elizabeth and dating from around 1600. Towards the end of her reign, subjects expressed their devotion to their queen in many different forms of popular arts and crafts.

Above and opposite A sixteenth-century portrait by an unknown English artist, thought to be of Elizabeth. Before and after her death, portraits such as this were said to be of the Queen. The authenticity of these claims is often difficult to prove, but adds all the more to their charm. This delightful portrait is proudly displayed in the great hall at Parham in West Sussex.

shall get by her death, and too slow for that good which shall get by her releasement from pains and misery.' He tried rousing her spirits with amusing verses, to which she smiled but said, 'When thou dost feel creeping time at thy gate, these fooleries will please thee less: I am past my relish for such matters.' Then her health rallied for a time and she was able to enjoy much of the seasonal festivities.

After a warning from Dr John Dee to beware of Whitehall Palace, Queen Elizabeth left on a stormy 18 January 1603 for her warmer residence of Richmond. It was an extremely cold winter, yet in February the Queen wore 'summerlike' garments, flaunting her regal style for an envoy from Venice. She dressed in a plunging-necked gown of silver and white taffeta trimmed with gold. 'Her hair was of a light colour never made by nature, and she wore great pearls like pears round the forehead. She had a vast quantity of gems and pearls upon her person; even under her stomacher she was covered with golden jewelled girdles and single gems, carbuncles, balas-rubies [delicate rose-pink rubies] and diamonds. Round her wrists in place of bracelets she wore double rows of pearls of more than medium size'; on her head, she wore an imperial crown. Having taken in this vision, the Venetian envoy received a scolding, for Venice had sent no resident ambassador to England throughout the whole of Elizabeth's reign. She reproached him for the discourtesy: 'Nor am I aware that my sex has brought me this demerit, for my sex cannot diminish my prestige, nor offend them who treat me as other princes are treated.' It was Elizabeth's last swagger.

A week or two later one of her remaining close friends, the Countess of Nottingham, granddaughter of Elizabeth's aunt, Mary Boleyn, died. Elizabeth lapsed into melancholia, becoming feverish and unable to sleep or eat. In March, Lady Nottingham's brother Robert Carey came to Richmond, where he found the Queen in her chamber seated on a pile of cushions, drained of her old sparkle, and at times as listless as if she were in a trance. She went on in this way for days until it became obvious the Queen was failing. 'Madame, to content the people you must go to bed', urged Sir Robert Cecil. But she would not be moved. 'Little man, little man, the word *must* is not to be used to Princes.' When Carey tried to raise her spirits, she took his hand and wrung it hard. 'No, Robin!', she pleaded, 'I am not well', and heaved 'forty or fifty great sighs'. Carey was grieved, 'for in all my lifetime before', he said, 'I never knew her fetch a sigh, but when the Queen of Scots was beheaded'.

On 21 March, Queen Elizabeth, by now in a very weakened condition, was finally persuaded to be carried to bed. Her coronation ring had grown into her flesh and had to be cut from her finger. Still, she would not name her successor. By the 23rd, an inflammation in her throat had made it difficult for her to speak. Robert Cecil begged her to give a sign nominating James VI as the next ruler of England. Lifting both her hands she made her fingers into the shape of a crown, then raised her hands to her head. The Archbishop of Canterbury, John Whitgift, arrived at Richmond Palace at six o'clock on the evening of 23 March, and remained on his knees praying and holding Elizabeth's hand until she sank into unconsciousness; everyone left the room except her chaplain Dr Parry and a few of her ladies. The Queen died between two and three o'clock the next morning, the 24th, 'mildly like a lamb, easily like a ripe apple from the tree'. Father Weston, a Catholic priest then imprisoned in the Tower of London, said that during the last days as the Queen lay dying 'a strange silence descended on the whole city ... not a bell rang out, not a bugle sounded'.

Elizabeth's body was taken to Westminster Palace, where it lay in state until the funeral ceremony. The Privy Council waited upon her with all the usual ceremony, 'the same expenditure, down to her very household and table service, as though she were not wrapped in many a fold of cerecloth, and hid in such a heap of lead, of coffin of pall, but was walking as she used to do at this season about the alleys of her gardens'. The Queen's body was eventually laid to rest in Westminster Abbey. An engraving was published with the inscription:

This Maiden Queen Elizabeth came into this world the Eve of the Nativity of the Blessed Virgin Mary, and died on the Eve of the Annunciation of the Virgin Mary.

Representations of her tomb were erected at numerous churches. The verses beneath the tomb erected at St Saviour's, Southwark, read:

This was she that in despight of death
Lives still ador'd ...

The new king ordered the funeral ceremony to be abridged, and wore no mourning, even though, it was observed, 'the Queen wore strick mourning when she took the life of his mother'. But then he was a king who disliked women, and one who lacked a sense of decorum – which had become so essential to Elizabeth.

At his coronation, James VI, now James I of England, made himself ridiculous, creating an excessive number of knights, some worthy, 'but with them … a skumm of suche as it wolde make a man sycke to thinke of', and from whom he extracted a large fee for bestowing the honour. His Court festivities dissolved into drunken scenes of debauchery. Even Sir John Harington, who enjoyed life to the full, and felt at ease in most circumstances, was appalled by the degeneration in Court behaviour. He did, however, appreciate the lavishness of the masques and the astounding costumes, sets and stage machinery designed by Inigo Jones. In 1606, he wrote: 'I have much marvelled at these strange pegeantries, and they do bring to my remembrance what passed of this sort in our Queen's days; of which I was sometime a humble presenter and assistant.' But then, 'I neer did see such lack of good order, discretion, and sobriety, as I have now done.' Inigo Jones was commissioned by the King to tear down Elizabeth's banqueting house at Whitehall, and replace it with a new, more solid building. What Jones created is undeniably elegant, an academic exercise in pure Renaissance style transplanted from Italy; but in comparison to what existed before, it is scalpelled clean of frivolity and emotion.

On 29 June 1613, the Globe Theatre was destroyed when its thatched roof became ignited by the discharge of a cannon during a performance of William Shakespeare's *King Henry VIII*. The play had been written either at the very end of Elizabeth's reign or in the early years of James's, although it was not published until 1623. In it, Shakespeare raises the issue of Elizabeth's legitimacy by putting the proceedings of Henry's separation from Catherine of Aragon in a doubtful light. He then flatters Elizabeth in the last scene of the play, Princess Elizabeth's Christening Ceremony, with comments on the fortuitous event, and anticipates the attitude of future generations towards Queen Elizabeth. Archbishop Cranmer is present – as he was at the real ceremony – but in Shakespeare's version Henry VIII also attends and makes an important contribution to the occasion. In addition, the scene includes a complimentary address to King James I. Archbishop Cranmer speaks:

This royal infant, (heaven still move about her!)
Though in her cradle, yet now promises
Upon this land a thousand thousand blessings …
She shall be lov'd and fear'd: her own shall bless her;
Her foes shake like a field of beaten corn,
And hang their heads with sorrow: good grows with her:
In her days every man shall eat in safety
Under his own vine, what he plants; and sing
The merry songs of peace to all his neighbours …
Nor shall this peace sleep with her: but as when
The bird of wonder dies, the maiden phoenix,
Her ashes new create another heir,
    As great in admiration as herself;
    So shall she leave her blessedness to one,
    (When heaven shall call her from this cloud of darkness)
    Who from the sacred ashes of her honour
Shall star-like rise, as great in fame as she was,
She shall be, to the happiness of England,
An aged princess; many days shall see her,
And yet no day without a deed to crown it.
Would I had known no more! but she must die –
She must, the saints must have her – yet a virgin …

King Henry responded:

O Lord archbishop,
Thou hast made me now a man! never, before
This happy child, did I get any thing:
This oracle of comfort has so pleased me,
That when I am in heaven I shall desire
To see what this child does, and praise my Maker.

It was not only Shakespeare and other Englishmen who applauded the reign of Queen Elizabeth. There were also many foreign tributes both during and after her lifetime. Perhaps the most satisfying to Elizabeth would have been the

Above Elizabeth's coat of arms were added to Parham in the early twentieth century. The Queen had visited the house briefly in 1593. In the nineteenth and early twentieth centuries, when the cult of Elizabeth was revived, people sought to advertise and exploit their Elizabethan connections.

estimation of Pope Sixtus V, who had urged Philip II to launch the Armada against England: 'She is certainly a great Queen and were she only a Catholic she would be our dearly beloved. Just look how well she governs! She is only a woman, only mistress of half an island, and yet she makes herself feared by Spain, by France, by the Empire, by all.' And the Spanish author Miguel de Cervantes paid a tribute to Elizabeth in his volume of short stories *Novelas ejemplares*, which was published in 1613: he referred to England as 'the famous Northern Island', governed 'by a most noble Queen'.

In England, as King James's popularity declined, Elizabeth was increasingly idolized. She became 'Saint Elizabeth' – 'in earth the first, in heaven the second Maid' – and the Elizabethan era became a vanished golden age. After the first decade of James's rule it was clear the reign of Elizabeth would not be forgotten. 'No Oblivion shall ever bury the Glory of her Name', wrote historian William Camden in the seventeenth century, 'for her happy and reknowned Memory still liveth, and shall for ever live in the Minds of men to all Posterity, as of one who … in Wisdome and Felicity of Government surpassed … all the Princes since the days of Augustus.' Other historians of the seventeenth, eighteenth and nineteenth centuries also praised her reign.

In 1821, George IV chose to wear for his coronation ceremony in Westminster Abbey an Elizabethan ruff and trunk hose, as did all his privy councillors. Sir Walter Scott reported that the occasion 'threw into the shade all scenes of similar magnificence, from the Field of the Cloth of Gold down to the present day'. After the ceremony, a thousand guests sat down to a revival of the coronation banquet in Westminster Hall, during which the King's Champion, dressed in armour and mounted upon a lavishly caparisoned steed, burst into the hall and made the traditional challenge.

That George IV revived the Elizabethan style for his coronation is not surprising: it was the style of England's glorious past, the style of a Protestant nation. A distrust of Catholics and Catholic countries had become widespread during the decades of war with France, 1793–1815, an attitude reflected in the popular Gothic novels of the period. Works by Mary Shelley, M C Lewis, Horace Walpole, Ann Radcliffe and others portrayed evil monks, the supernatural and wicked doings in medieval castles, often set in the countries of southern Europe. This anti-Catholic mood, combined with the rapid social change taking place throughout the country, caused by the Industrial Revolution, produced a nostalgia for the past, particularly for the era of Queen

Elizabeth, when the Church of England had become firmly established, and the Spanish foe – perpetrators of the Inquisition – had been vanquished.

Nostalgia for the Elizabethan past was similarly evident in architecture, becoming a symbol during the nineteenth century of a patriotic romance with the long-dead Queen and the golden age when England was 'merrie'. In 1833, T H Clarke's *Domestic Architecture in the Reigns of Queen Elizabeth and James I* was published, and 1835 saw the publication of J Hakewill's *Attempt to determine the Exact Character of Elizabethan Architecture,* its title suggesting the complex nature of the style. The year 1835 was also the one in which, according to architectural historian Timothy Mowl, 'Elizabethan' was declared an acceptable style for the new Palace of Westminster, Britain's seat of government. Between 1837 and 1841, various books on Elizabethan architecture were published, including *Studies From Old English Mansions*, *Details of Elizabethan Architecture* and the four volumes of *Mansions of England in the Olden Time*. The latter, by Joseph Nash, was a fantasy tour of houses and palaces such as Hampton Court, Wollaton Hall and Hardwick Hall, and included an illustration of a cosy Elizabethan family scene set in Leicester's gatehouse at Kenilworth Castle, depicting a baby in a cradle and a little boy playing soldier, while mother spins wool and father dozes by the fire.

Queen Elizabeth and Elizabethan style had become an industry. Across Britain, owners of grand country houses began searching for links with Elizabeth, and the innumerable beds that she is supposed to have slept in began to appear. Her emblems and coat of arms were emblazoned over entrances, on chimney-pieces, ceilings, windows and staircases. Those with genuine late sixteenth-century houses unpicked their modern additions. Others created new sprawling wonders with vast bay windows, elaborate porches, loggias and turreted roofs displaying heraldic beasts brandishing their gilded vanes and flags skywards. Topiary again appeared in gardens, wherein banqueting houses were built as a decorative feature. The interiors of these new or renewed Elizabethan houses were filled with sixteenth-century antiques, furniture passed off as antiques of the period, or new furnishings of sixteenth-century design. During the nineteenth and twentieth centuries, manufacturers' pattern books and catalogues exhibited fabrics, wallpapers, curtains, mirrors and tables of Elizabethan design, along with chairs and sofas of gilded wood and rich crimson-coloured upholstery.

The fashion for Elizabethan interiors was soon followed by a craze for displaying armour; chivalry became a popular theme in literature, while the tilt was also revived. In 1838, Samuel Pratt, a dealer in armoury, opened showrooms in Lower Grosvenor Street, London, for the hire and sale of suits of armour, tents, shields, crests, pavilions, stands and all the other paraphernalia required for the tilt-yard. In August of that year, fifty-five lords and ladies, distinguished guests and members of the public travelled from all over the British Isles, and from Calcutta, Copenhagen, Rio de Janeiro, America and France, to the castle of Lord Eglinton in Ayrshire, where thirteen knights in ceremonial armour broke lances against each other for a prize from the Queen of Beauty, Lady Seymour. Among the combatants at Eglinton's tilt were Francis Hopkins, Knight of the Burning Tower, and Charles Lamb, Knight of the White Rose, who wore a single white rose in his cap and displayed the motto '*Une seule*' ('Only one') on his belt 'all in token of hys Lady Love'. Lord Eglinton himself was clad in gold. It was fun, it was nonsense, it was also patriotic – nationalism again being equated with love for Elizabeth and the Elizabethan. For those who crossed the globe to be there, it may also have been the pursuit of an idealistic dream.

By 1868, some three hundred years after Queen Elizabeth succeeded to the throne, the chivalrous ideal associated with her and immortalized in Spenser's *The Faerie Queen* had evidently penetrated the hearts and minds of Englishmen, for in that year Prime Minister Benjamin Disraeli, with the flair of a true Elizabethan courtier, knelt down and kissed the hand of Queen Victoria, pledging 'loving loyalty and faith'. By the 1870s, he was calling her 'the Faery' – she appreciated the accolade.

But after all, perhaps the best proof that Elizabeth had attained the objective she had sought – the adulation of the English people – is the fact that her speech to Parliament in 1601 became known as the 'Golden Speech', and that it has been read and reread by the nation in times of crisis. From that speech the words most frequently quoted are:

… though God hath raised me high, yet this I count
the glory of my crown, that I have reigned with your loves.

At the same time, she achieved a style that was, and is, uniquely hers.

Elizabeth Tudor's Life: A Chronology

1527   Henry VIII seeks an annulment of his marriage to Catherine of Aragon

1529–1534   Royal Supremacy and Reformation

1533   Henry VIII marries Anne Boleyn, 25 January; Archbishop Cranmer judges the marriage of Henry VIII and Catherine of Aragon invalid, 23 May; coronation of Queen Anne, 1 June; birth of Elizabeth Tudor, 7 September

1534   Pope Clement VII declares marriage of Henry VIII and Catherine of Aragon valid, 23 March

1536–1539   Dissolution of the monasteries

1536   Death of Catherine of Aragon, 7 January; marriage of Henry VIII and Anne Boleyn declared null and void, 17 May; execution of Anne Boleyn, 19 May; Henry VIII marries Jane Seymour, 30 May

1537   Birth of Lady Jane Grey, early October; birth of Edward Tudor, 12 October; death of Jane Seymour, 24 October

1540   Henry VIII marries Anne of Cleves, 6 January; marriage of Henry VIII and Anne of Cleves declared null and void, 9 July; Henry VIII marries Katherine Howard, 28 July

1542   Execution of Katherine Howard, 13 February; birth of Mary Stuart, 8 December; death of James V of Scotland, 14 December; Mary Stuart becomes Queen of Scots

1543   Henry VIII marries Katherine Parr, 12 July

1547   Death of Henry VIII, 28 January; accession of Edward VI; Edward Seymour, Duke of Somerset, made Lord Protector, 16 February; Lord High Admiral Sir Thomas Seymour raises the possibility of marriage to Elizabeth; Katherine Parr marries Thomas Seymour, probably in May; Seymour begins flirtation with Elizabeth

1548   Mary, Queen of Scots taken to France and betrothed to Francis the Dauphin, heir to the French throne; death of Katherine Parr, 7 September

1549   Sir Thomas Seymour arrested, 17 January; Elizabeth interrogated; First Act of Uniformity; execution of Thomas Seymour, 20 March; fall of Lord Protector Somerset

1550   John Dudley, Earl of Warwick, later Duke of Northumberland, made President of the Privy Council, and effectively Lord Protector; Sir Robert Dudley marries Amy Robsart, 4 June

1552   Execution of Somerset, 22 January; Second Act of Uniformity

1553   Lady Jane Grey marries Guildford Dudley, 21 May; Edward VI's 'Device' of the Crown in favour of Lady Jane Grey, 14 June; death of Edward VI, 6 July; Lady Jane Grey proclaimed queen, 9 July; accession of Mary I, 19 July; execution of Northumberland, 22 August; Mary I marries Philip II of Spain by proxy, October

1554   Publication of marriage treaty between Mary and Philip II; Thomas Wyatt's rebellion, 25 January; execution of Lady Jane Grey and Guildford Dudley, 12 February; Elizabeth imprisoned in the Tower, March; Wyatt executed, April; Elizabeth imprisoned at Woodstock, 23 May; Philip II arrives in England, July; his marriage to Mary I is celebrated; Cardinal Pole arrives in England to reconcile the country to the Pope

1555   Elizabeth released from Woodstock, 17 April; persecution of 'heretics' begins

1556   Archbishop Cranmer burned at the stake, 21 March; Sir Thomas Pope sent to Hatfield as Elizabeth's custodian, June

1557   England declares war on France

1558   Mary, Queen of Scots marries Francis the Dauphin, 24 April; loss of Calais to the French; death of Mary I; accession of Elizabeth I, 17 November; William Cecil appointed Elizabeth's Principal Secretary of State; Robert Dudley made Master of the Queen's Horse

1559   Coronation of Elizabeth I, 15 January; Treaty of Cateau-Cambrésis between England, France and Spain; death of Henry II of France; accession of Francis II, husband of Mary, Queen of Scots; Acts of Uniformity and Supremacy

1560   Death of Francis II, 5 December; accession of Charles IX; Catherine de' Medici becomes Regent; death of Amy Robsart, 8 September

1561   Mary returns to Scotland, August

1562   Elizabeth seriously ill with smallpox

1564   Robert Dudley created Earl of Leicester and proposed as husband for Mary, Queen of Scots; Christopher Hatton appointed a gentleman pensioner; William Shakespeare born

1565   Mary, Queen of Scots marries Lord Darnley, July

1566   Birth of James VI of Scotland, later James I of England, June

1567   Murder of Lord Darnley, 10 February; marriage of Mary and Earl of Bothwell, 16 May; Mary's abdication; Robert Devereux, later 2nd Earl of Essex, born, 10 November

1568   Mary flees to England, and is placed under arrest

1569   Proposed marriage of Mary and Norfolk; the rebellion of the Northern earls

1570   Papal bull of excommunication against Elizabeth

1571   Ridolfi plot; William Cecil created Lord Burghley

1572   Execution of Norfolk; St Bartholomew's Day massacre of Protestants in France

1574   Death of Charles IX and accession of Henry III

1577   Francis Drake's voyage of circumnavigation; Hatton made Vice-Chamberlain and knighted

1578   Leicester marries Lettice Knollys; marriage negotiations with the Duke of Alençon begin

1579   Alençon's brief visit to England

1580   Return of Francis Drake from voyage

1581   Sir Henry Lee initiates the Accession Day tilts; Drake knighted; Alençon returns to England and stays for three months

1582   Walter Ralegh joins the Court

1583   Throckmorton plot

1584   Death of Alençon, 10 June; Ralegh knighted

1585   Establishment of the Roanoke Colony in Virginia, America

1586   Babington plot; trial of Mary, Queen of Scots; death of Sir Philip Sidney

1587   Execution of Mary, Queen of Scots, 8 February; Sir Christopher Hatton made Lord Chancellor; Essex made Master of the Horse

1588   Defeat of the Spanish Armada; death of the Earl of Leicester, 4 September

1590   Sir Henry Lee resigns as Queen's Champion to George Clifford, 3rd Earl of Cumberland; Essex marries Frances, widow of Sir Philip Sidney

1591   Death of Sir Christopher Hatton

1595   Death of Sir Francis Drake

1596   Robert Cecil appointed Secretary of State

1598   Death of Philip II; death of Lord Burghley

1601   Rebellion of the Earl of Essex, 8 February; execution of Essex, 25 February

1603   Death of Elizabeth, 24 March; accession of James I, son of Mary, Queen of Scots

Directory of Elizabethan Houses and Design

The following is a list of Elizabethan palaces, castles and houses that are open to the public. For more information on these and other Elizabethan houses, consult *Hudson's Historic Houses and Gardens*.

Eltham Palace
Court Yard
Eltham SE9 5QE
020 8294 2548
Medieval great hall

Hampton Court
East Molesey
Surrey KT8 9AU
020 8781 9500
Henry VIII's apartments; royal chapel; great hall; Tudor kitchens; paintings; tapestries; gardens

Hatfield Old Palace – the remaining wing is located within the grounds of:
Hatfield House
Hatfield
Hertfordshire AL9 5NQ
01707 262823
Great hall of the Old Palace and gardens. In Hatfield House: paintings; tapestries; objects and clothing associated with Elizabeth

Nonsuch palace – no longer exists, however items reputedly from Nonsuch and furnishings associated with Elizabeth can be seen at:
Loseley Park
Guildford
Surrey GU3 1HS
01483 304440

Displays on Nonsuch can also be seen at:
Whitehall
1 Malden Road
Cheam
Surrey SM3 8QD
020 8643 1236

Tower of London
London EC3N 2AB
020 7709 0765
Castle; royal armouries; crown jewels

Whitehall Palace – no longer exists, however the Banqueting Hall built by Inigo Jones to replace Elizabeth's banqueting house is open to the public:
Banqueting Hall
Whitehall
London SW1A 2ER
020 7930 4179

Windsor Castle
Windsor
Berkshire SL4 1NJ
01753 868286
Paintings; furnishings

Audley End House
Audley End
Saffron Walden
Essex CB11 4JF
01799 522399
An indication of the grandeur of Theobalds

Berkeley Castle
Berkeley
Gloucestershire GL13 9BQ
01453 810332
Castle; park; Elizabeth's bedcover; paintings

Burghley House
Stamford
Lincolnshire PE9 3JY
01780 752451
The country seat of William Cecil, Lord Burghley; house; paintings; items associated with Elizabeth and furnishings associated with Mary, Queen of Scots

Hardwick Hall
Doe Lea
Chesterfield
Derbyshire S44 5QJ
01246 850430
House; tapestries, garden; paintings; decorative plaster-work; furniture; furnishings associated with Elizabeth and Mary, Queen of Scots

Hardwick Old Hall
Doe Lea
Chesterfield
Derbyshire S44 5QJ
01246 850431
Decorative plaster-work; ruins

Holdenby House
Holdenby
Northamptonshire NN6 8DJ
01604 770074
House; garden; ruins; paintings; drawings; falconry centre; armoury; chapel

Kenilworth Castle
Kenilworth
Warwickshire CV8 1NE
01926 852078
Castle; garden; great hall where Elizabeth dined; wing Leicester built for Elizabeth; gatehouse

Kirby Hall
Deene
Corby
Northamptonshire NN17 5EN
01536 203230
The most romantic – visit during the morning or late afternoon, and do not be put off by the reception committee of peacocks

Lyveden New Bield
Near Oundle
Peterborough
Northamptonshire PE8 5AT
01832 205358
Water gardens

Sudeley Castle
Winchcombe
Near Cheltenham
Gloucestershire GL54 5JD
01242 603197
Castle; gardens; castle church where Katherine Parr is buried; paintings; drawings; objects associated with Elizabeth; needlework of Anne Boleyn

Warwick Castle
Warwick CV34 4QU
01926 406600
Castle, grounds; paintings; Kenilworth buffet; Elizabeth's saddle and other objects associated with Elizabeth

Wollaton Hall
Wollaton Park
Nottingham
Nottinghamshire NG22 8PQ
0115 928 1333
Now a natural history museum, but well worth a visit

Museums

The museums listed below contain collections of Elizabethan and sixteenth-century furniture, fittings, artefacts, paintings, costume, textiles and jewellery. For more detailed information consult *Museums and Galleries of Great Britain and Ireland*; *The Cambridge Guide to the Museums of Europe*; and *The Official Museum Directory*, published for the American Association of Museums.

Ashmolean Museum
Beaumont Street
Oxford OX1 2PH
01685 278000

The Baltimore Museum of Art
Art Museum Drive
Baltimore, Maryland 21218-3898
(410) 396 6300

British Museum
Great Russell Street
London WC1B 3DG
020 7636 1555

Burrell Collection
Pollok Country Park
2060 Pollokshaws Road
Glasgow G43 1AT
0141 649 7151

Cooper-Hewitt National Design Museum
Smithsonian Institution
2 East 91st Street
New York 10128
(212) 860 6868

J Paul Getty Museum
1200 Getty Center Drive
Suite 1000
Los Angeles
California 90049-1687
(310) 459 7611

Metropolitan Museum of Art
5th Avenue at 82nd Street
New York 10028
(212) 879 5500

Musée du Louvre
Palais du Louvre
75041 Paris
(1) 42603926

Museum of Costume
Assembly Rooms
Bennett Street
Bath
Avon BA1 2QH
01225 461111

Museum of London
London Wall
London EC2Y 5HN
020 7600 3699

National Gallery
Trafalgar Square
London WC2N 5DN
020 7839 3321

National Portrait Gallery
St Martin's Place
London WC2H 0HE
020 7306 0055

National Maritime Museum
Romney Road
London SE10 9NF
020 8858 4422

Victoria and Albert Museum
Cromwell Road
London SW7 2RL
020 7938 8500

Walker Art Gallery
William Brown Street
Liverpool L3 8EL
0151 478 4199

Elizabethan Design

The following are just a few of the many companies manufacturing designs from the Elizabethan era.

★ indicates only available to the trade

Fabric and Wallpaper

Alexander Beauchamp Wallpaper and Fabrics Ltd
Hall Lane
Rhos, Wrexham LL14 1TG
01978 844442

Sanderson
Chalfont House
Oxford Road
Denham, Middlesex UB9 4DX
01895 830044

Bennison Fabrics
16 Holbein Place
London SW1W 8NL
020 7730 8076

★Clarence House
211 East 58th Street
New York 10022
(212) 752 2890

Cole & Son (Wallpaper) Ltd
Chelsea Harbour Design Centre
London SW10 0XE
020 7607 4288

★Fabricut
9303 East 46th Street
Tulsa, Oklahoma 74145
(918) 622 7700

Hamilton Weston Wallpapers Ltd
18 St Mary's Grove
Richmond
Surrey TW9 1UY
020 8940 4850

John Oliver
33 Pembridge Road
Notting Hill
London W11 3HG
020 7221 6466

★Schumacher
79 Madison Avenue
New York 10016
(212) 213 7978

★S Harris
930 East 46th Street
Tulsa, Oklahoma 74145
(918) 622 7700

Furniture

Bylaw Furniture
The Workshop
Norwich Road
Lenwade
Norwich
Norfolk NR9 5SH
01603 308090

Titchmarsh & Goodwin
Unit 2
Chelsea Harbour
London SW10
020 7376 7567

Directory of Elizabethan Houses and Design

Bibliography

Andrews, Martin, 'Theobalds Palace: the Gardens and the Park', *Garden History*, Vol 21 No 2, Winter 1993

Aston, Margaret (ed), *The Panorama of the Renaissance*, 1996

Aubrey John, *Brief Lives*, 1693

Auerbach, Erna, *Paintings and Sculpture at Hatfield House*

Adams, C, *Kingsley*, 1971

Bell, Arthur, *The Royal Manor of Richmond*, 1907

Boulding, Anthony, *The History of Hampton Court Palace Gardens*, Hampton Court publication

Buxton, John, *Elizabethan Taste*, 1963

Camden, William, *The History of the Most Renowned and Victorious Princess Elizabeth, late Queen of England*, 1675

Cavallo, Adolph S, *Needlework*, 1979

Cawthorne, Nigel, *Sex Lives of the Kings and Queens of England* 1994

Chambers, E K, *Sir Henry Lee*, 1936

Chapman, Frederic, *Ancient Royal Palaces in and near London*, 1902

Collins, A Jefferies, *Jewels and Plate of Queen Elizabeth I: The Inventory of 1574*, 1955

Colvin, H (ed), *The History of the King's Works*, 1976

Croft-Murray, E, 'Decorative Painting in England 1537–1837', Vol 1, *Country Life*, limited edition, 1962

Cunningham, P (ed), *Extracts from the Accounts of the Revels at Court*, 1842

Dalton, Christopher, 'All Saints' Church, Holdenby, Northamptonshire', The Redundant Churches Fund, 1993

Deacon, Richard, *John Dee*, 1968

Dent, John, *The Quest for Nonsuch*, 1962

Digby, *Elizabethan Embroidery*, 1963

Dovey, Zillah, *An Elizabethan Progress*, 1996

Dunlop, Ian, *Palaces and Progresses of Elizabeth I*, 1962

Elton, G R, *England under the Tudors*, 1997

Elvetham: An Account of Queen Elizabeth's visit there in 1591, privately printed

Erickson, Carolly, *The First Elizabeth*, 1983

Evans, Joan, *English Jewellery*, 1921

Falkus, Christopher (ed), *The Private Lives of the Tudor Monarchs* 1974

Feuillerat, Albert (ed), *Documents Relating to the Office of the Revels*, 1908

Foister, Susan, 'Paintings and other Works of Art in Sixteenth-Century English Inventories', *Burlington Magazine*, Vol CXIII, 1981, pp 273–82

Fraser, Antonia, *The Six Wives of Henry VIII*, 1992

Fuller, Thomas, Freeman, John (ed), *The Worthies of England*, 1952

Furnivall, F J (ed), *A Description of England, 1577*, 1877

Gascoigne, George, *The Princely Pleasures of Kenilworth*, 1576, reprinted 1821

Giles, J A (ed), *The Whole Works of Roger Ascham*, 1865

Gilmore Vines, Alice, *Neither Fire or Steel*, 1978

Girouard, Mark, 'Acrobatic Gothic', *Country Life*, 31 December 1970, pp 1282–6

Girouard, Mark, *Life in the English Country House*, 1978

Girouard, Mark, 'Elizabethan Holdenby', *Country Life*, 18 October 1979, pp 1288, and 25 October 1979, p 1400

Girouard, Mark, *The Return to Camelot: Chivalry and the English Gentleman*, 1981

Girouard, Mark, *Robert Smythson and the Elizabethan Country House*, 1983

Girouard, Mark, 'Still Waters Run Deep', *Country Life*, 11 February 1993, pp 46–9

Groos, G W (ed), *The Diary of Baron Waldstein*, 1981

Guy, John, *Tudor England*, 1988

Hamilton Hill, Margot and Bucknell, Peter A, *The Evolution of Fashion*, 1967

Harris, Nicolas, *Memoirs of the Life and Times of Sir Christopher Hatton*, 1847

Hartshorne, E, *Memorials of Holdenby*, 1867

Harrison, G B (ed), *The Letters of Queen Elizabeth*, 1935

Hearn, Karen (ed), *Dynasties: Painting in Tudor and Jacobean England, 1530–1630*, 1995

Henderson, Pamela 'Sir Francis Bacon's Water Gardens at Gorhambury', *Garden History*, Vol 20 No 2, 1992

Hibbert, Christopher, *The English: A Social History 1066–1945*, 1988

Holinshed, R, *Chronicles of England, Scotland and Ireland*, 1807/8

Howard, Maurice, *The Tudor Image*, 1995

Jackson-Stops, Gervase and Pipkin, James, *The Treasure Houses of Britain: Five Hundred Years of Private Patronage and Art Collecting*, 1985

Jenkins, Elizabeth, *Elizabeth the Great*, 1958

Jenkins, Elizabeth, *Elizabeth and Leicester*, 1961

Johnson, Paul, *Elizabeth I*, 1974

Kelly, Francis M, 'Queen Elizabeth and her Dresses', *Connoisseur*, CXIII, 1944, pp 71–8

Klarwill, Victor von, *Queen Elizabeth and her Foreigners*, (translated by Professor T H Nash), 1928

Knowles, E H, *The Castle of Kenilworth*, 1872

Lacy, Robert, *The Life and Times of Henry VIII*, 1972

Laneham, Robert, Furnivall F J (ed), *Robert Laneham's Letter Describing a Part of the Entertainment unto Queen Elizabeth at the Castle of Kenilworth, 1575*, 1907

Laungervyle Society Reprints, 'Hentzner's Travels', pp 31–80, privately printed, 1881–2

Law, Ernest, *The History of Hampton Court Palace*, Vol 1, 1890

Lloyd, Christopher, *The Royal Collection*, 1992

Luke, Mary, *The Nine Days Queen*, 1986

Marshall, Pamela, *Wollaton Hall: An Archaeological Survey*, 1996

Mason, A E W, *The Life of Francis Drake*, 1943

Millar, Oliver, 'The Inventories and Valuations of the King's Goods', Walpole Society, XLIII, 1972

Millar, Oliver (ed), *The Pictures in the Collection of Her Majesty the Queen: The Tudor, Stuart and Early Georgian Pictures*, 1963

Morrill, John (ed), *The Oxford Illustrated History of Tudor and Stuart Britain*, 1996

Mowl, Timothy, *Elizabethan and Jacobean Style*, 1993

Nash, Joseph, Anderson, J Corbet (ed), *Mansions of England in the Olden Time*, 1871

Naunton, Sir Robert, Cerovski, John S (ed), *Fragmenta Regalia*, 1641

Neale, J E, *Queen Elizabeth*, 1934

Neale, Sir John, *Queen Elizabeth I*, 1952

Neale, Sir John, *Elizabeth I and her Parliaments*, 1953

Needham, R, *Somerset House Past and Present*, 1905

Nichols, John, *The Progresses and Public Processions of Queen Elizabeth*, Vol 1 and 2, 1788; Vol 3, 1805

Norton Anthology of English Literature, 1962

Osborne, June, *Entertaining Elizabeth I*, 1989

Peck, Francis, *Desiderata Curiosa*, 1732

Perry, Maria, *Elizabeth I*, 1990

Rawson, Maud Stepney, *Bess of Hardwick and her Circle*, 1910

Ridley, Jasper, *The Tudor Age*, 1988

Robinson, John Mardin, *Windsor Castle*, 1996

Routh, C R N, *Who's Who in Tudor England*, 1990

Rowse, A L, *The England of Elizabeth*, 1950

Rowse, A L, *Raleigh and the Throckmortons*, 1962

Rowse, A L, *The Elizabethan Renaissance: The Life of the Society*, 1971

Rowse, A L, *The Elizabethan Renaissance: The Cultural Achievement*, 1972

Shakespeare's England, Vols 1 & 2, 1916

Sheppard, Edgar, *Memorials of St James's Palace*, Vol 1, 1894

Sheppard, E, *The Old Royal Palace of Whitehall*, 1902

Sotheby's, *English Silver Treasures from the Kremlin: A Loan Exhibition*, 1991

Starkey, David, *The English Court from the Wars of the Roses to the Civil War*, 1987

Staunton, Howard (ed), *The Complete Illustrated Shakespeare*, 1979

Steele, M S, *Plays and Masques at Court during the Reigns of Elizabeth, James I and Charles I*, 1920

Strong, Roy, *Portraits of Queen Elizabeth I*, 1963

Strong, Roy, *The English Icon*, 1969

Strong, Roy, *The Cult of Elizabeth*, 1977

Strong, Roy, *The Renaissance Garden in England*, 1979

Strong, Roy, *Art and Power: Renaissance Festivals 1450–1650*, 1984

Strong, Roy, *Gloriana: The Portraits of Queen Elizabeth I*, 1987

Strong, Roy, *Lost Treasures of Britain*, 1990

Strong, Roy, *The Tudor and Stuart Monarchy: Pageantry, Painting, Iconography*, 1995

Strong, Roy, 'More Tudor Artists', *Burlington Magazine*, February 1996, CVIII, pp 83–5

Strong, Roy and Trevelyan Oman, Julia, *Elizabeth R*, 1971

Summerson, John, *Architecture in Britain*, 1953

Summerson, John, 'The Building of Theobalds 1564–1585', *Archaeologia*, XCVII, 1959, pp 107–26

Tighe, Robert R and Davis, James E, *The Annals of Windsor*, 2 vols, 1858

Thomson, W G, *A History of Tapestry*, 1906

Thurley, Simon, *The Royal Palaces of Tudor England*, 1993

Williams, Clare, *Thomas Platter's Travels in England, 1599*, 1937

Williams, Neville, *All the Queen's Men*, 1972

Williams, Neville, *The Life and Times of Elizabeth I*, 1972

Williams, Penry, *The Later Tudors*, 1995

Yates, Frances A, 'Elizabethan Chivalry: The Romance of the Accession Day Tilts', *Journal of the Warburg and Courtauld Institutes*, XX, 1957, pp 4–25

Yates, Frances A, *Astraea: The Imperial Theme in the Sixteenth Century*, 1975

Also

Public Record Office:
PRO E101/429/3 – Accounts of the Exchequer (Coronation); PRO E407/4 – fragments of accounts; PRO E407/56 – fragments of accounts; PRO SP12/24 ff 107; PRO LC9/62, f 7 – 'Garderoba Magna, Regina Eliz'; PRO LC2, LC5

Calendar of State Papers:
CSP Spanish, 1568–79, pp 121–33, 404, 405; CSP 1558–80, pp 27, 53–84; CSP Domestic Elizabeth 1581–90, no 46

Northamptonshire Record Office:
Finch Hatton MS 617 and 618; Hatton MS 3713

Bodleian Library, Oxford:
MS Cherry 36; MS e Musaeo 242; MS Rowl 85

MSS The Marquess of Salisbury:
CP 140/94; 143/46; 143/48; 143/62; HMC Salisbury MSS, Vol XIV, pp 76–8; HMC NRA 32925 Gascoigne-Cecil

Acknowledgments

I would like to pay tribute to A L Rowse for his dedication to the study of Elizabeth and the Elizabethan era, and whose works have given me worlds to ponder; he is greatly missed. I would also like to thank Roz Osinski for her tireless help and assistance; Dr Susan Foister for kindly reading the text and offering suggestions; Robin Harcourt Williams for his help and expert transcriptions of Hatfield papers; Marcus Lynch for his kind assistance, and for supplying me with copies of documents regarding Elizabeth's visit to Warwick Castle, and also Corrina Jacob; Jon Culverhouse, Burghley House, for his help and assistance; Paul Wallace-Stock for the information he provided and for allowing us to photograph Elvetham Hall; Mr and Mrs James Lowther for their hospitality and kindness in allowing us to photograph Holdenby House; Michael More Molyneux for his assistance and kindness in allowing us to take photographs at Loseley Hall; Pat Kennedy for her help and kindness in allowing us to take photographs at Parham. With special thanks also to the Marquess of Salisbury for permission to take photographs at Hatfield House and Old Palace; Lady Ashcombe, Sudeley Castle; Lord and Lady Tollemache; John Cockcroft and the Nottinghamshire County Council, Wollaton Hall; Gill Harrison and Historic Royal Palaces, the Tower of London and Hampton Court; the Southampton City Council, the Tudor House; English Heritage, Kenilworth Castle, Hardwick Old Hall, Bolsover Castle and Kirby Hall; the National Trust for allowing us to photograph Melford Hall; Also Vanessa Pintado of the Pierpont Morgan Library in New York; the staff of the Northamptonshire County Records Office; the archivists of the British Library, the Bodleian Library, the Ashmolean Museum, and the staff of the London Library. Finally, I would like to thank Sir Roy Strong, Dr Mark Girouard, and Timothy Mowl for their works, which have inspired me, and of course, my husband, for without him nothing is possible.

Illustration Credits

By courtesy of the Marquess of Salisbury: 2, 3, 84, 85; by courtesy of the National Portrait Gallery, London: 6, 7, 46, 47, 89, 119, 157, 160; V & A Picture Library: 16, 117, 158, 159, 195; Bodleian Library, Oxford: 17, 37, 38, 153; British Library: 19, 68, 73, 98, 99, 101, 120; by gracious permission of Her Majesty the Queen: 20, 21, 64–5; Sir John Soane's Museum: 32, 33, 108, 114, 132; British Museum: 34, 162, 163; Museum of the History of Science, Oxford: 39; Berkeley Castle/Bridgeman Art Library, London: 50; Private Collection/Bridgeman Art Library London: 51; by kind permission of Viscount De L'Isle: 54, 55; Fitzwilliam Museum, University of Cambridge/Bridgeman Art Library, London: 62; British Museum/Bridgeman Art Library, London: 72; Walker Art Gallery, Liverpool/Bridgeman Art Library, London: 74; Ashmolean Museum, Oxford: 76, 77, 167; Royal Horticultural Society: 78, 116; Victoria and Albert Museum/Bridgeman Art Library, London: 79; Philip Mould, Historical Portraits Ltd, London/Bridgeman Art Library, London: 80 (bottom left), 81; by kind permission of the Marquess of Tavistock and the Trustees of the Bedford Estate: Endpapers, 82, 83, 166; the Duke of Devonshire and the Trustees of the Chatsworth Settlement: 130; National Trust Picture Library: 148, 149, 150, 154; by kind permission of Warwick Castle: 172, 173, 177; English Heritage Photographic Library: 174; St Faith's Church, King's Lynn, Norfolk/Bridgeman Art Library, London: 179; National Maritime Museum, Greenwich: 188; College of Arms: 189; Museum of London: 191

Index